Life Masterpiece

Jim Lutes

Life Masterpiece

Jim Lutes

Jim Lutes

Life Masterpiece

ISBN-13: 978-1-4951-4658-9

Contents

Foreword

Everywhere I turn, people from all walks of like are experiencing stress, anxiety, fear, anger, money concerns, and what seems to them to be insurmountable challenges and conflicts in the way they live their lives. And the harsh reality is that most search all their lives trying to find the answers.

How about you? Have you ever ached emotionally? Have you ever experienced pain that was non-physical, but were unable to pinpoint exactly where it hurts? Have you ever experienced a feeling of total loneliness or emptiness, like there was no one there for you? Maybe you've felt those emotional aches like a deep void, and no matter how hard you tried, you couldn't fill the void, or find a remedy for the ache.

Or for many, because it hurts too much to feel, they completely suppress their feelings and shut down, and now function in survival mode.

If any of the above sounds familiar, it doesn't have to be that way for you because you are about to discover some answers within the pages of this book.

Jim Lutes has dedicated the last 30 years of his life to studying the human mind and emotions, and why we do what we do. His understanding of how the subconscious mind is programmed, and more importantly how to re-program it, is unsurpassed.

In today's world, it is essential for all of us to unravel old patterns of belief and to train our minds to function in new ways. As you read, you will feel like a mental switch has been thrown, old programs and beliefs will be erased, and new ones will take their place.

I have known Jim Lutes and his work for over 15 years. He has helped tens of thousands to overcome their limiting beliefs and to reprogram their subconscious for success and happiness. The insights contained within these pages gives you practical tools for managing your mind, your emotions, and your life.

I've worked with Tony Robbins, Jim Rohn, T. Harv Eker, Zig Ziglar, Brian Tracy, and others in the personal development business. Jim is right up there amongst the best.

Personally, I have dedicated the last 40 years to the personal empowerment business helping more than a million people to improve their lives and businesses. I would be the last to lead you to believe that the tools and strategies within these pages will solve all your problems, or that you won't need to do anything else after reading this book. The journey of life and the challenges and problems we are faced with along the way are ongoing. I know that from using these principles in my own life. Jim Lutes simply provides you with some practical tools to help guide you through your challenges, allowing you to live a life filled with more of what you do want and less of what you don't want.

Enjoy the journey! And be prepared because your life is about to change!

Jim Britt ~ Author, *Rings of Truth*

Part 1: Universal Power

Introduction

For as long as I can remember, I've been completely fascinated by the human mind. From a very young age, I've been enthralled with what I perceived to be the complex and fantastical workings of the human mind. As a young boy, I would watch people that were intensely focused and achieving great things, and see people that overcame great odds, and many times what I observed prompted me to take an introspective look at myself—even as a young person—and wonder why I wasn't achieving great things in my own life, and how I might be able to attain that level of focus and achievement. Rather than discard it as something that was impossible for me, I sought to figure out why it was possible for these people.

Many years ago, when I was twelve years old, a friend of mine had a skin condition. He would visit the dermatologist time and time again, and the dermatologist would take care of the skin condition using conventional dermatological methods. Behind closed doors, however, the dermatologist recommended that my friend see a hypnotist. I remember the incident clearly: I distinctly recall my friend coming back after three or four sessions with the hypnotist, and his skin was perfectly clear and it was free of whatever the disorder was. This incident only served to pique my ever-growing curiosity and fascination with the human mind, because now

I had seen that someone who was not a medical doctor, operating on the physical level only, had completely healed my friend of his condition.

I want to share with you a story that was a turning point in my own journey on the road to success. This incident served to further solidify my interest in the human mind and our capacity to work with it. When I was in my early twenties, I was sitting one day on a wall by the beach in San Diego. While I was sitting there, I met a gentleman who I guessed to be around forty in age. We struck up conversation, and in the course of that conversation, I asked him what he did for a living. He told me he was an entrepreneur.

Back then, I had no idea what the word "entrepreneur" even was, so I asked him to elaborate. He said, "Well, I decide where I go 365, 24/7. I decided to use my mind outside the normal academic construct." And in that moment, it hit me. I saw that because my father was a businessman and my brother was a doctor, they had limitations on their lifestyles based on what they did for work. I'm not saying those are not admirable career paths—not at all. I was singularly struck by being an entrepreneur, however, and by the idea of being able to determine, shape, and create my own life. It sounded like freedom to me, so much so that I knew in that moment that I wanted it for myself.

I asked this gentleman, "What's the secret?" This is what he told me: First, you build yourself and then you build your life. Let me tell you, if I could find this gentleman today, I would buy him a brand new car because that was one of those aha moments that changed the course of my life forever. I asked him to elaborate on what he meant by "build yourself," and his reply was this: You build your mind. You build your mind into an unstoppable force. You build your mind using strategies and tactics to do so. He went on to reference some of the major books that were out at the time, such as *Think and Grow Rich* and *The Magic of Believing*, to name a few. I began to study and study, and I engaged even more deeply with my initial interest in the human mind because now I actually had material that explained a lot of what I was so fascinated with as a younger man.

Much of the material I was reading kept mentioning things called the "subconscious," the "super-conscious," and the "universal conscious." I saw some redundancy and repetition in their explanations in many different ways. Then, as fate would have it, I went to a party one evening, and a hypnotist was there. I was in awe, because again I heard this word "subconscious," and it was being used by the hypnotist. I pulled him aside, and I told him I thought what he had done was absolutely fascinating. It is fascinating; as I look back, I can clearly see how my interest as a young boy, marveling at how people achieved things using their minds, led me to meeting an individual that explained to me that he had achieved his goals by building his mind, which led me to finding the key phrases and words in books through my self-study, which led me to a party where I found this gentleman who was quite skilled at hypnosis and who pointed me in the direction of where I could learn it, too. I asked this gentleman who the best hypnotists in the world were, and I had the good fortune to be able to study under them from a very early age. As I began to do so, I began to develop and expand upon what I was taught, and literally worked with thousands and thousands of people, both individually and in seminars and large groups.

Like anything else, with practice you become skilled at what you do. I was so thoroughly fascinated and enthralled by this topic that this translated into me studying absolutely everything on the subject that I could find. I studied everyone I could find until I embarked on a full-blown career on the study of the human mind, using a whole host of modalities and techniques. Some of these included psychosomatic parenthetics, high-level hypnosis, Ericksonian hypnosis, neuro-linguistic programming, and a variety of other techniques, some of which I merged and created into my own protocols.

I'm a firm believer, obviously, based on my background, that when you look at your life unfold, the work of dealing with your own mind is what allows you to amplify or increase your confidence, self-esteem and self-image (which are, really, the core of everything), and diminish the fears, doubts, and hesitations. In the course of my studies, I began to teach other people. I found that I had a natural ability to convey complex subjects of the human mind and, let's face it, the mind is a complex thing. Now, I'm not trying to impress the psychological community out there, but I do want to help individuals to acquire, assimilate, and apply these strategies to their own lives. Because of this, it's been a very rewarding career, and it continues to be so. I would venture to say that no strategy or tactic out there is more powerful than the combination of these strategies that are drawn from years of experience and expertise.

When it comes to living our lives, we so often seek answers outside of ourselves as to how we can achieve all that we desire. We are looking for happiness, wealth, peace, good health, and great relationships. In effect, we really want it all. If we really want all these things in life, why is it so difficult to obtain them? Why does it feel like a perpetual struggle to find fulfillment in life?

I believe that we have an inherent sticking point within us that keeps us in struggle, and keeps us in the state of non-achievement. The clincher is that this same force that keeps us in struggle is the same force that can lift and propel us out of the struggle.

The concept that I am talking about is essentially this: Our lives are the product of our thoughts and beliefs. Just like the gentleman on the beach told me that fateful day in San Diego, first you build yourself, then you build your life. This book will take this concept and deepen your understanding of it, through explaining how our minds work and offering effective expert techniques and strategies to help shift limiting thoughts and beliefs. Our relationship to our thoughts is pivotal to how our lives express themselves. I will show you step-by-step methods that will reveal how your mind is working moment to moment, and how to successfully link into the potential that is waiting for you. You have the power to create a rich and satisfying life. You don't need to call yourself 'spiritual' to be able to grasp this concept. This book will empower you with skills and approaches to master the relationship between your mind and your lived experience, giving you the ingenuity to create a life you love, starting now.

For centuries, spiritual teachers and seekers around the world have been drawn to finding solutions to ease human suffering. Being human, it seems, has been marked by the experience of suffering. We have come to know this well through the stories of Plato, the Buddha, Jesus, Krishna, Lao-tse, Mohammed, and Rudolf Steiner, to name a few. In the early 20th century, several Western writers and thinkers, coming from non-spiritual and even non-scientific backgrounds, began to disclose their findings and ideas around what keeps us in struggle, and how to get out of it. Writers like U.S. Anderson, Wallace Wattles, and, more notably, Napoleon Hill all elaborated upon the concept of how to be a success through managing our thoughts, and in so doing echoed the wisdom of spiritual teachers. These writers attempted to bring these concepts to the general public; however, most folks haven't heard of these philosophers. I believe that if these writers and their ideas had become popular at the time they were developing, we would be living in a much different world today, one that is not characterized by so much struggle and strife.

Throughout the following chapters, I will take you on a journey through the workings of the conscious and subconscious minds. In section one, you will learn about Universal Power, the subconscious mind, and the profound connection between the two. I will explain the difference between the subconscious and conscious minds. You will read a simplistic explanation of the brain and how it affects your subconscious and conscious mind. You will see how your mind was blank at birth, and was programmed through the three formative avenues of trauma, authority figures, and repetition. You will also learn how, from this programming, limiting beliefs formed and how these contribute to a running dialogue in your conscious mind, which is not of service to you. You will also learn about the ego and the role it plays in your thinking patterns and life choices. Further, you will see how this all impacts your self-esteem, and learn how you can actually escape the trap of low self-esteem, recognizing that this, too, is a choice you are capable of making. At the end of section one, I introduce the notion that you are creation, that Universal Power surrounds and is in you, accessed via the subconscious mind. I discuss ideas and their genesis, and also how you can make this concept work for you as you design your Life Masterpiece.

In section two, we build on section one as I reveal how you have the potential, much like everyone else in the world, to redirect your life at any moment. You will learn how your internal world affects your external environment, and why you really are the "other people." In this section, we talk about the importance of living in the now—because life is precious and short. I encourage you to get to work now on your mind—as the life you've always dreamed of is just waiting for you to create it.

In section three, we get into the nitty-gritty of my techniques and strategies for really working with the mind. You will learn about hypnosis, via a cursory overview, and the truth about the power of suggestion. You will learn concrete tools in this section to adjust your mind, including visualizing when your brain is in the alpha state, future-pacing, and controlling your internal and external environments. In this section, I share my eight Rules of the Mind, matching them to their corresponding Universal Laws so that you can build upon them as you begin to apply them in your life. We discuss the power of emotional expectation, and what it means to emotionalize your thoughts and desires, along with why this is important. Finally, in section three, you will receive the technique that is essential to making all of the strategies taught in this section work for you in a profound way.

Of course, you can't just learn strategies without a roadmap to show you how best to apply these. This is what section four is about. This section will give you the steps to apply all the tools from section three in the primary areas people wish to change: Health, Relationships, and Finances. This is where you can see the potential of what section three is teaching, and get a sense of what to expect when you actually start to apply and implement the strategies you are learning.

In section five, I take you a little deeper into some of the overall concepts introduced throughout the book. These ideas are a little more advanced, and I am sharing them to get you moving through the beginner stages of this work, through intermediate and into some advanced learning when it comes to harnessing the power of the mind. In this section I discuss the unexplored territory that is your mind, as well as intuition, what it is, where it comes from—and how to use it in concert with all of these other tools.

Finally, we wrap up the book with an encouraging chapter to pump you up and remind you that you can do this work—and the rewards that are waiting for you once you do. After reading this book, which I hope you will read again and again, you will have a solid handle on how to work with your mind in ways that will alter your life completely and profoundly for the better.

Your life is your work of art, and you are the master creator. Consider your life like a blank canvas, your life experiences like a box of the most exquisite paints, and the paintbrush like the pointed arrow of your polished mind. You literally hold in your hands (and your mind) the power to execute your life as a masterpiece of art. As you begin to absorb the concept that your thoughts create your reality, you will begin to see life differently and your relationship and impact on your life will shift. As you practice and work with the techniques I show you, you will begin to see how much power your thoughts have, and how they directly influence your experience of life. As you become aware of this phenomenon, you will notice yourself paying much more attention to your thoughts in order to better be able to shift them, thus influencing your life in ways that you desire.

The technology is not new, and it has never really been a secret, despite what people believe. Seekers, scientists, and writers for centuries have known that there is something much bigger surrounding us, encompassing us, creating us, that indeed we came from that which surrounds and encompasses us. This 'something' is what I call Universal Power. When we are caught up in the mundane activities of day-to-day life, sometimes even hyper-focused on survival, we easily forget that there is a larger force at play in our lives. We are so distracted, we miss out on connecting to this 'larger-than-ourselves' force that permeates all facets of life, including our own. We disregard, or perhaps are truly unaware, that we were created from Universal Power, and as such we are the essence of Universal Power.

Consider the metaphoric example of the ocean. Whales, dolphins, sea lions, octopuses, starfish, crustaceans, spades of sea plants, jellyfish, water, minerals, sea horses, down to the tiniest single-celled sea creatures all live in the medium we know as the ocean. The sea is much like the all-encompassing life force that unites and supports all of the living things that derive their life sustenance through the existence of the ocean. In this way, all of the creatures and plants that live in the ocean are connected to one another, even though they may not be conscious of this fact. Can you imagine your own life as part of a larger nexus of all living things? If we can truly start to see who we are within this bigger picture, and how we are essentially part of all that surrounds us, then we can really begin to shape our lives the way we want to.

I invite you to join me on a journey to the center of your power: Your mind. If you are feeling dissatisfied with your life and know you are ready to make some lasting changes, this book will serve as a powerful start to creating the life you wish to lead. Open your mind and your heart, and get ready to learn how you can start living your Life Masterpiece.

Chapter One: Universal Power

Have you ever questioned why some people in the world achieve their dreams and reach the pinnacles of success, while others struggle and suffer throughout life? Have you ever seen a moral, upright, honest citizen just barely scraping by, while someone who engages in unethical and sometimes criminal behavior is a millionaire? Have you wondered why or how this might be? Have you read book after book about the Law of Attraction or the secrets to manifesting the life you want, only to find they still did not help you bring about change within yourself?

The concepts I am going to share with you in this book are all simple and relevant, and geared towards helping you effect change in your life at the deepest level. Would you believe me if I said that you already have everything inside you that you need to create the life you are dreaming of? What so many people before me have alluded to being a secret, I am going to blast out into the open. You have access to far greater knowledge and capability than you can imagine, and I can show you the key to accessing this. Once you understand and acknowledge your connection with Universal Power, you will see what an ally you have. After many years of working in the personal development field and as a hypnotist, I have seen the evidence of this Universal Power in action, and how making use of it truly changes lives.

Over time, I have studied various interpretations of the rules of the mind, and I have narrowed these down to eight key rules. As you read through this book, you will become intimately familiar with these rules. The first and most primary of these rules is this: Every thought creates an organic response. Some people learn this theoretically, and some folks just know it. Never underestimate the power that you will have when you learn the strategies and techniques I share in this book. Learning these techniques puts you in a very specialized group of people that have learned to use their mind in a skillful and powerful way. This group includes people who practice meditation. These people recognize that meditation is an absolutely incredible practice, and that focusing and bringing the mind to one-pointed attention is a powerful skill to learn. The same goes for anyone who chooses to use a different modality to clear their mind or become more mindful. With the current rise in the popularity of mindfulness practice, it is evident that people are catching on to the value in learning these practices. However, the strategies that you will learn in Life Masterpiece are dynamic strategies. They are directive strategies. They are tools that you can actually use while you're in a state of mindfulness to create organic change, to create mental change, to create emotional change, and to create physical change.

You have the ability to actually craft yourself, your existence, and your interactions with other people into a truly built-by-design blueprint for your life. It's in your very own hands and no one else's! Imagine you were building a house. You would never build a house haphazardly. Yet we end up being born and just hope that our house functions. We have a physical need to keep our body functioning perfectly, yet mentally and emotionally we run all over the place. We become victims of circumstance, of our programming, of our traumatic incidents, of our repetitions. To utilize strategies like the ones I will explain in Part Three is to keep a strong holistic foundation on all four planes of existence: mental, emotional, physical, and spiritual. It just comes down to common sense. The challenge is that most people have never learned what I teach. Most people have never even learned other strategies, much less applied or become skilled at them.

Once you become skillful with these strategies, you truly have power over the control center in your mind. You become the pilot of your life, sitting at the cockpit of your own mind. You can go into your mind and adjust the speed, the altitude, and the output, because it's not on autopilot anymore. You're now controlling the cockpit, setting those coordinates. Using these techniques, you can go ahead and flip the autopilot off. Of course, you still have to know where you are going before you take yourself off of autopilot. Too often, people are on autopilot heading towards a destination when they'll suddenly crash into a mountain because they had no idea where their destination was. Clarity of outcome is number one. Combine this with the strategies and the blueprint of exactly where you want to go and that will take you there.

The key to unlocking the vault of your entire being—and to creating lasting change and eradicating limiting beliefs from your life—lies within you. Your subconscious mind is the most powerful force in the universe, and making it an ally instead of an adversary will lead you to finding freedom from defeating, limiting, unhelpful behaviors, thought patterns, and beliefs. The truth is that you are already in possession of everything you need to create the life you dream of.

The concept that we are the creators of our own lives is not new; however, it is not widely believed by everyone, and it's certainly not taught in schools! Have you ever felt like you were the victim of circumstances outside of your control? I am sure that we all have, from time to time. What we so often fail to realize is that even in those circumstances, indeed, in any circumstance, we still always have choice. Believe it or not, we are always playing an active role in the outcome of our situation. Let me explain this for you: Most of our choices are born from our previous life experiences and how they have affected us. The experiences we have in our early years create patterns and it is from these patterns that we make decisions as we move through life. More commonly than not, we make choices and decisions, to the tune of several hundred each day, without even consciously thinking about them. When I ask people about their belief systems and the habits and patterns that basically control their lives, I am often struck by how few of these beliefs and habits were ever chosen by that person on a conscious level.

In other words, the rules that are guiding your life about how to live your own life are very often picked up unconsciously. When we make decisions from an unconscious level, we are often making decisions that are reactionary or habitual in nature. In this way, we aren't acting as active agents of our life experiences—we are unconsciously making choices and decisions as though we were still living in our past. Effectively, we are re-creating our past, remapping it onto our present (and future) life experiences.

Let me tell you the story of one of my clients, whom I'll call 'Ellie,' to give you an example of this phenomenon in action. Ellie is a 45-year-old white woman who lives in a well-known North American city. Ellie has been married three times. Each of her marriages has ended in bitter divorces, which have left her, in some instances, very nearly penniless. Ellie came to me after her third divorce, completely beside herself with grief and depression. She repeatedly asked, "Why does this keep happening to me?" During a hypnosis session with Ellie, it was discovered that she had been physically abused by her stepfather as a little girl. Through several sessions together, we discovered that Ellie was carrying a belief in her subconscious mind that she didn't deserve a healthy relationship with a 'good' man. In fact, deep down, she didn't believe herself to deserve love from anyone. Ellie made the connection that she had been choosing men who resembled her step-father (bitter, controlling, withholding of affection) and perpetually trying to please and appease them, often at the expense of her own self. Even though Ellie said to herself, "I don't want to have these same kinds of unhealthy relationships," she was still effectively reinforcing this concept in her own mind through underlying beliefs and thought patterns she did not realize were running in the background. Once Ellie realized that her words and thoughts were unconsciously coming from her past, effectively being made from the perspective of the scared little girl, she decided it was time to make a change. Ellie and I worked together using hypnosis and the techniques outlined in this book to reprogram her sense of herself. I also helped Ellie to really feel and visualize what a healthy relationship looked and felt like. We focused on what Ellie wanted and what her desired outcome was instead of what she did not want. Ellie began to feel stronger, more confident, and more powerful and even began to feel more loveable.

Through Ellie's practice of the methods I will show you, she came to understand the importance of shifting her old beliefs and thoughts to enable her the freedom to change the course of her relationships. She was able to begin to live a life full of more contentment, with more connection to her inner world. She aligned herself with her subconscious mind so that she could become the 'captain' of her own life-ship. Ellie stopped seeking men to make her feel good about herself and began to attract men who wanted to be with the beautiful being that she had become.

If you want to create a life that is all you have dreamed of, it is essential that you learn to reprogram your mind so that you become conscious about your choices, instead of operating within the same patterns generated by your subconscious.

Let me back it all up for a moment here and explain a few basic things. A simplistic view of the mind reveals it is composed of two facets: The conscious and the subconscious. I would like to point out that often the words "subconscious" and "unconscious" are used interchangeably to mean the same thing, namely that facet of the mind which lies beneath the conscious mind. In my work, I use the word subconscious, and this is the language I will be using throughout the book. Regardless of what you know and believe about unconscious and subconscious, it is really only a difference of semantics when it comes down to definition and role.

The conscious mind is largely in charge of logic, rational thinking, and decision- making. The conscious mind also includes memories, perceptions, and feelings that are in our awareness in the present moment. The conscious mind is also responsible for bodily actions you do with intention while in a conscious state, like when you choose to move your hands, or walk, or dance. The conscious mind also acts as a filter for the mind, and will filter beliefs you hear in a conscious state according to whether or not they match beliefs that are already entrenched in your subconscious mind.

The subconscious mind is much more creative than we realize, and more creative than the conscious mind. The subconscious mind is also where emotions live. The subconscious mind not only controls our emotions, but is also the storehouse for our beliefs and memories. The subconscious mind is also responsible for bodily actions that take place involuntarily, such as breathing. The subconscious is also where we are connected to the universal consciousness, what I call Universal Power. Remember that example of the ocean? The subconscious mind is like this, an expression of the multi-faceted super-connected universe.

Whether you are a spiritual person or not, there is evidence from both the scientific and spiritual sides claiming that our subconscious is directly connected to all the wisdom of the universe, Universal Power; what some people like to refer to as God.   Indeed, we are created out of this Universal Power—we are just as much a part of creation as the trees, the birds, the ocean. If you want even basic evidence that we are created of Universal Power and that our access to it is through the subconscious mind, consider this: The subconscious mind keeps our bodies alive—it keeps us breathing when we sleep, and allows our bodies to respond appropriately when in danger.   We don't think about breathing, it happens. Is that from your conscious choosing? No—it's the subconscious, the part of you that is nature, that is the universe, and that is an active cog in the machine of Universal Power. Have you ever found yourself in a dangerous situation, for example an encounter with a bear, and felt as though 'you' were not making the decisions in that moment? Did it feel as though another 'force' was acting through you in your encounter with the bear? Surely, you've heard people tell similar stories about dangerous encounters, in the wild or otherwise. You may have heard folks say, "I don't know what made me fight back in the bear encounter," or, "It didn't feel like I was the one deciding in that moment." This is yet another example of the subconscious mind at work. It is this life force that wants to keep us alive and safe at all times.

The subconscious mind contains patterns from generations upon generations of human evolution that replay through our own responses to events in our lives.

Have you ever had a premonition, or a flash of intuition about an event in your life? That was evidence of the subconscious mind and the potential it allows you. If you grow your intuitive muscle, it can develop into innate wisdom beyond what your conscious mind could possibly possess. This innate wisdom is also Universal Power, for Universal Power is all of the intelligence of our universe of creation. Knowing that you are a part of all of creation through your subconscious mind is an incredibly empowering thought shift to make. It is also integral to practicing any kind of techniques that invite you to shift your thoughts and belief patterns. Whether you want to call it God, the Universe, Source, or need to understand it from a scientific purview, the truth is that the creation and expansion of the entire universe we live in, a universe made up of matter and energy, is accessible through your subconscious mind. It informs everything we do; we live and breathe Universal Power. It is not something you go out and buy, it is not something some people have and others don't, and I would even venture so far as to say it is not something we can even try to not believe in. It is not woo-woo, it is not even a solely spiritual concept; rather, it is a fact.

For centuries, thinkers both science-minded and spiritual-minded have acknowledged and expanded upon the concept that the Universe is creation, and we are part of creation. The part of us as humans that links us to the divine oneness, the Universal Power, is held in our subconscious mind. You can see now why the mind is so fascinating, right? You can spin this concept any way you like to fit Christian, Hindu, Jewish, Buddhist, or Gurdjieffian paradigms of thinking, or invite the Quantum Physicists to the table, but I encourage you not to deny its validity. I encourage you to see for yourself how you can access and use this Universal Power to design your life the way you dream it to be. Doing this will take you from being a TV-watching couch potato cynic who believes they are stuck in this lifestyle forever, to being a bold, truly abundant, energetic individual who is fully empowered to embrace all of life in its richness. This one shift takes you out of victimhood and directly into the driver's seat of your life.

Despite being the seat of all the intelligence of the universe, Universal Power, the subconscious mind still gets its orders from the conscious mind. Imagine your mind, comprised of both the conscious and subconscious, is like a manufacturing company: The boss gives the orders, and the workers manufacture the goods. The workers, however, don't ask questions—they get the orders, and they get to work. So it is with the subconscious mind—it gets the 'orders' from the conscious mind, and gets to work. The subconscious mind hears neither the subtleties of the orders nor the negations, but it works hard to provide what the conscious mind is looking for. This is why when you repeat a phrase like, "I can't afford it" in your conscious mind, the subconscious works hard to keep you unable to afford things. Or when you think "I don't want to be poor," regardless of the word "don't" in that phrase, the subconscious will get busy working to bring you more poverty. The subconscious mind will do whatever it takes to generate the result of the thought of the conscious mind. Hence, keeping positive and affirming thoughts present in your conscious mind is essential. Affirmations only work on the conscious level, and even then are still subject to being filtered by the subconscious mind if they don't match the belief already in place. This is why emotionalizing the desired outcome and attaching the desired result to powerful imagery is so important.

You are the creator of your life. Your thoughts—and particularly the visual and emotional element that accompany your thoughts—serve to create your day-to-day experience. Do you want a life that is a stick figure drawing, or a plain old paint-by-numbers creation? Or are you someone yearning to create a vibrant masterpiece of a life, filled with all of the dreams you long for?

When you were a child, your identity formed and, for most of us, this identity was formed out of the stories about ourselves that our families or other significant people told us. Our identities formed at the level of the subconscious, and our conscious minds held onto these identities, which in turn infused our egos. I tend to think of identity and ego as two sides of the same coin; essentially both are constructs that our minds devised to help us respond to our lives in a way that keeps us safe. Our identities formed out of our early life experiences and the decisions we made to help get our needs met and survive our childhoods. I believe identity is the strongest force in the human personality. Believe it or not, what shapes you the most is not your capability, but your identity. When I say identity, I mean the rules you have created to support who you *think* you are. The problem is that most of us defined ourselves a long time ago. Because we defined our identities a long time ago, as we grew into adulthood, it may have become more and more evident that they no longer really fit who we have grown into. Then, when we try to step outside these definitions, we become really uncomfortable.

There is a strong pull in the human personality to remain consistent, and, thanks to this pull, we long to remain consistent with how we define ourselves. In the Western world, in particular, it seems we are strongly influenced and encouraged to behave with consistency, routine and predictability. As human beings of the West, we are saddled with resistance to change, both internally and externally. One of the deepest human needs we have is for certainty, and, if this is the case and we do not know who we are, then we do not know how to act. We start to define ourselves early on, and tell ourselves stories to go along with the definition, stories like "I'm ugly" or "I'm a loser" or "I can't catch a break" and others along those lines. We don't always recognize when we have grown out of these stories, and instead we let them linger on in our thoughts. We stay in an outdated identity because we love consistency and certainty. It gives us a sense of safety and predictability that matches nicely with the status quo. We don't have to get caught up in these stories and have them taint our lives any longer! We can reprogram our minds and step out of limiting beliefs, re-creating our identities to match who we have evolved to become in our lives.

Before we get into reprogramming our minds, however, let's go back to the beginning. How did limiting thoughts and beliefs even get into our minds? How did our identities become defined? How is our sense of 'self' created?

Without going into too much detail, I want to explain in a simple way the different levels on which the brain functions. Our brains operate on four different wavelengths—alpha, beta, theta, and delta. The alpha level is the level we pass through to go to sleep, and to wake up again, and is the most common level the brain is in when one is in a trance state. We are relaxed in this state, and our brain activity slows. At the same time, we are more creative in this state. Also, there is the propensity for fears to dissipate while the brain is at the alpha level, and generally a feeling of contentment is present.

The beta level is the level in which adult brains operate most of the time, when we are awake. This is when our eyes are focused, our conscious mind is in control, and we are thinking in a logical way. We are alert, able to concentrate, and focused. If you have to give a presentation, run a race or prepare for an exam, this is the state you want your brain functioning in.

The theta level is in action during states of deeper trance, or dreaming. Our brain activity is much slower in this state, slowing almost to the same rate as when it is asleep. This state is expansive and is much more attuned with the subconscious. While the brain is in this state, it can reveal stored memories and intuitive flashes. This is the level of the brain most commonly associated with deep states of meditation. We are more responsive to suggestions and information when we are in this state, for suggestions induced while in the theta state will be absorbed by the subconscious mind. This is what makes hypnosis so effective as a change-agent for people.

The delta level is in operation during deep sleep. This is the slowest of our brain frequencies. Being in the delta level is very effective for helping with any healing process. Just notice people who do not get into this state because they lack deep sleep—you will observe they lack the same energy, vitality, and brain power overall to get through each day. Time spent with our brains in a delta state can be extremely regenerative for our bodies; it can also help us open up to our intuition and tap into the Universal Power held in the subconscious mind.

As children, our brains tend to operate out of the alpha state the majority of the time. When we are in the alpha state, we are highly receptive. The messages we take in while in this level go straight to our subconscious mind. This explains why children are so impressionable. Our parents, and other significant people from our childhood, had a tremendous impact on the messages that our subconscious minds received. Events from our childhood played a strong role in the development of our self-image, our identity and our overall evolution into adulthood.

To take this back to identity, hopefully now the picture is becoming clearer that you may or may not have had as much control over your identity as you believe you do now. What you absorbed as a child had everything to do with shaping your identity, not to mention framing the choices and decisions you continue to make in your adult life today.

This is why we find ourselves in a position where we live life a particular way. We believe we were raised in a particular way, and so we act in a way that matches these early experiences and habits that have now become a set of expectations. Throughout our lives, in an effort to avoid pain and continue to meet our needs, we made critical decisions about who we are and how we thought we needed to be. We believe we know who we are, but the way we have behaved for years is simply a series of adaptations. It was just something that happened as we were trying to get our basic needs met; as we were trying to get the love, respect, or acceptance from a parent, sibling, peer, lover, or other loved one. This caused us to make key decisions that enabled us to adapt to the circumstances around us. We may not realize for years that we have become experts at living in our identities, despite the fact that these identities do not reflect our true nature, but rather the conditioning and other influences we were raised with. So many ideas and beliefs that were never even ours passed into our minds from the moment we were born, and so many of these served to help us get our needs met through childhood and adolescence. Much of these ideas and beliefs have become more and more obsolete as we move through adulthood. Even if you feel like you held your own when you were growing up, and that the relationships you had as a child, especially with your mother and father, were strong, and you feel like you are strong as a result, there are still patterns your subconscious mind is running that no longer serve you. It is the experience of having to deal with all of the events of your past—and this includes events that may have happened before you were born, in your parents' past—all of these events affect your ability to make decisions, your health, your relationships, your finances, your choices, your behaviors, and the general circumstances of your life, even today.

In order to move into the fullness of our potential, we have to be able to clear out the beliefs and thoughts that are negative and are no longer needed. First, it is necessary to identify what these limiting thoughts and beliefs are. In order to create your masterpiece, you have to learn how to take care of the big things—like each of the colors in your crayon box—and align the mental, emotional, financial, relationship, and spiritual aspects of yourself.

Chapter Two: The Blank Canvas

We are all born of pure spirit. Our subconscious mind is the gateway to the universe and connection with the divine. Intuition is like the conversation between 'ourselves' and universal consciousness. When we talk of being intuitive and accessing intuition, we are talking about using that part of the subconscious mind that *is* Universal Power. This happens when all of our 'parts' are in alignment. I'll talk about the different parts of ourselves a little later in the book.

We are all equals when we are first born—regardless of what kind of family or situation we are born into, the truth is we are still vulnerable, pure, needy babies. Our minds are like a blank canvas, ready to learn and grow and not pre-programmed in any way. At this stage, we are residing in a pure and innocent state, if you will. We soak up knowledge at a fast and furious pace in the first months and years of our lives, as our canvas becomes painted on with the impressions of our parents, caregivers, guardians, other family and other authority figures in our lives. Consequently, as we soak up knowledge and imprinted programming from our parents and everyone else who affects us, our intuition is weakened, and our connection to the greater subconscious mind of the entire universe is lost. We are conditioned to rely more on external factors and cues in our environment then we are on our *internal* environment.

What starts out as the blank canvas quickly becomes crowded with programming, right from the minute we are born. There are three primary ways our minds get programmed as we grow up: Traumatic experience, authority figures, and repetition.

When you experience trauma as a child, your subconscious creates a response at the time with the primary goal of keeping you safe. For example, perhaps when you were four years old you burned your hand on the stove. This trauma and memory became stored in the subconscious and as you grew up, you knew not to put your hand on the stove. A more extreme example might suggest that you even became afraid of the stove as you grew older. Sometimes the trauma is no longer kept in your memory at the conscious level and you don't know why you have certain fears. You might have a strong fear of being in small spaces. What you may not even remember is an incident from your early childhood wherein you were contained in a small space and you were terrified. Programming from trauma is often forgotten by the conscious mind as people age, because of the emotional powerhouse traumatic incidents are. Our innate nature is so concerned with keeping us protected and safe that we may develop very strong emotional responses as a result of traumatic experiences. You can always find out what programming is running in your subconscious mind that came from trauma by working with a qualified hypnotist or psychotherapist.

The other way we become programmed is through the authority figures in our lives. Our parents are usually the major players here, however it can be anyone that was influential in your life as you grew up. For lots of people, if there are limiting beliefs or thoughts around money, chances are they came from the authority figures and the words they heard these figures say that they took in. If you grew up poor and always heard your father say, "Money doesn't grow on trees!" it is possible that you may grow up hoarding your money or believing you will never have enough. If your parents always asked you to be quiet or did not even invite you to speak at the dinner table as a child, you may have taken in the message that your feelings don't matter and you continue to keep quiet as you grow older, only to find that as an adult it keeps you from making presentations at work or limits you in other ways. The voices we hear growing up impact our subconscious minds in profound ways, and one could argue these have the strongest influence on what we believe about ourselves and the world. Again, the old internal versus external struggle. In contemporary Western society, we are much more encouraged to give more importance to the external messages, as opposed to listening to what our internal messages (intuition) are saying.

The third common way we are programmed is through repetition. Any words, comments, behaviors, or actions that were repeated to you as you grew up became entrenched in your subconscious mind, for better or for worse. A good example of repetition is the media. If you think back to all the messages you received as a child growing up—all of the gender messages, messages about how you should look, even how you should be if you want to "fit in," all of these are repeated over and over again through media programming, particularly television. These messages are usually reinforced by our family, authority figures, and society. If you don't believe you were programmed by television as a child, think again. For men and women, there are probably millions of cases of people struggling with low self-esteem as a direct result of images in the media of unattainable bodies and looks for the greater majority of people.

Whether this programming came to us as a result of traumatic episodes we faced as children, or from the voices of the authority figures in our lives, most of us grew into adults entirely unaware that there had been any programming altogether. The reality is, as you grew up, the authority figures—and even the media and other influential voices—helped you create parameters in your life. For example, the need for approval and the fear of criticism may have led you to slowly lose your individuality over the years, without your being consciously aware that it was happening. It's a subtle process that can effectively erode any 'authentic' or 'true' sense of self.

Instead of following your heart, you found yourself following the masses without ever fully understanding why. One day you arrived at the realization that you are dissatisfied, unhappy, and not fully self-expressed on the path you're living. In short, you recognize that you are living far under your potential. Yet chances are, even if you arrived to that point, you were still unable to comprehend why you felt that way or what hidden forces may have been at work to lead to that moment. You may not recall the specific words spoken by those around you that you absorbed as you were growing up, but they are affecting your life even now through the emotions that show up when you are involved in certain situations. Negative statements of any kind, like "you'll never amount to anything," "no one in our family is rich," "it's no use trying," "you will fail," "life is one big struggle" and so on were far more dangerous than those who uttered them could have anticipated. For these statements dug grooves in your subconscious mind, the repercussions of which persist throughout your life unless you learn to overcome them. If you have ever wondered why you felt anxiety or fear when you tried something new, or despair every time you look at your finances, chances are these emotions have arisen as a result of a belief being triggered by an earlier experience that you were not aware was still influencing your behavior. Are you beginning to 'see' how much your original blank canvas has been painted on by other people's ideas and influences?

If people only knew how influential their words are on their babies' minds, we would see a radical shift in the way we parent. The programming we received, especially in the earliest years of our lives, has a profound effect on who we are and the choices we make today. This is not to be used as an excuse to justify why you are stuck, or in bad relationships, sickly, or financially unstable. Rather, just recognizing that you began with a blank canvas that was subsequently influenced and programmed by everyone around you is an essential first step in moving you forward. You cannot move forward in life into the aligned and positive human you wish to be, manifesting all that you desire, without recognizing the areas your mind has been imprinted upon from an early age. This is a crucial ingredient to making lasting change and using those changes to fuel the life you desire to create.

We are born the same, all of us, coming into the world as babies with open and empty minds. As we grow up, we assimilate cultural norms, we assimilate the fears of our parents and other authority figures, and we assimilate the need for approval or fear of criticism, which can translate into the loss of our individuality. Have you ever felt out of alignment with who you really are? Chances are if you dig deep enough into your subconscious mind, you have some story in there that was put there by someone of authority in your life, and it's a fear of rejection, or a need for approval, or any other fear or idea that would contribute to you hiding your real self from the world. Somehow you learned it was not safe to be an individual, particularly the individual that you really are, and this learning has led you to where you are now. If you are stuck and out of alignment, feeling like one of the masses and locked into a 9-5 job while your heart screams for freedom and the ability to work for yourself, take a look at what conditions you grew up in, and whose voices and thoughts you heard most of. If we humans only knew the influence we have on one other, we would help each other to grow positive subconscious thought patterns, not limiting ones. Imagine what kind of world we would live in if this were the case.

Another way to look at this is to think of your mind as a nightclub. When you were a child, there was a bouncer at the door who let everyone in. You did not have a filter yet—in this case, a bouncer who was discerning. So everyone came in—negative thoughts, negative memories, positive thoughts, lessons learned, basically any and all experiences, both positive and negative. Everyone and everything got into your nightclub from the moment you were born. Now imagine that as you grew older, the bouncer decided to start to be more discerning about who is already in your nightclub. You might try to allow a new positive, affirming thought into your nightclub, only to find there is a nightclub full of negative memories, beliefs, and other thoughts that are crowding out the positive thoughts you are trying to re-populate your nightclub with.

As you start to change your life by changing your thoughts, it is imperative that you kick some of those dancers out of the nightclub. If you don't make space for some positive thoughts—or new thoughts at all—those thoughts cannot stay, because the nightclub is so full of negative thoughts. What happens next? You need to empty the whole nightclub, evict the negative thoughts and limiting beliefs, and start to only let the positive and affirming thoughts in. Does this make sense? The bouncer needs to wake up and actively guard the nightclub to only allow in those thoughts and beliefs that serve you. We go along in life and we often don't even want to see the occupants of our nightclub, sometimes going so far as to engage in self-medicating behavior so we can stay in denial. Many of us are afraid to "see" who has been populating our nightclub. Somehow a lot of the negative thoughts and beliefs that got into the nightclub serve us and have served us through the years, helping us to survive. Many of these thoughts and beliefs become patterns and give us a sense of safety and predictability, even though many of them are no longer helpful in our present lives. Just because our nightclub is populated by ideas and thoughts that previously helped us to navigate experiences in our lives, it doesn't mean they need to stay on! And, to boot, they are not the best dancers in the nightclub either!

While we are the chief creators of our lives, these patterns and much of our early conditioning may have led us to a place of feeling stuck, negative, or dissatisfied with our current lifestyle. Imagine for a moment that your life is like a car. Would you give the wheel to people you did not know or trust? Would you let a person who repeatedly crashed the car be the driver? No, of course not! Beginning to recognize and examine these negative thoughts, patterns, and beliefs will enable you to become the driver in your life. Paying attention to your thoughts moment to moment will empower you to navigate the terrain of your life with more skill, ease, and harmony.

Our subconscious mind absorbed everything when we were growing up; our canvas filled up quickly, whether we liked it or not. Now, as adults, it's important to dive deep into our subconscious minds to filter out all of the limiting beliefs—beliefs that perhaps once served us, long ago, but that certainly no longer serve us or our greater purpose in life. It's time for the nightclub bouncer to put his foot down, by being more selective and discerning about who is allowed to come into the nightclub. (Hint, you are the bouncer!)

It is incredible how common it is when people begin to reassess their lives and their relationships, with themselves and others, or the success they are having (or perhaps not having), that they discover that much of what has been negatively affecting their lives, their achievements, their finances, their careers, their intimate relationships, and even their bodies, was influenced by their parents. Not only have our parents programmed and imprinted their beliefs and patterns upon us, but we also developed strategies to cope with our living situations, the other side of this double-edged sword. As we grew up and tried to be liked, approved of, or appreciated by one or both parents, we developed behaviors, beliefs, and patterns to help us meet those needs. In many cases, the decisions people have made from childhood onward were about avoiding the pain that was inflicted on them by a parent or loved one. So we can be forty, fifty, even eighty years old, and we are still living the strategies we lived as children. We are effectively re-living the lives of our younger selves in a cycle of unconscious repetition.

As if these things weren't enough to leave us limited as adults, for many of us, as we grew up we often told ourselves "I'll never be like that!" when referring to our parents. Yet here you are today, quite possibly exactly like that. You don't want to admit it, but if you watched a film of your interactions, you might say, "Oh dear, I never wanted to be like that parent," yet you are. Or, if you didn't become the parent you said you would never become, you may have gone in the entirely opposite direction, and you are not like that parent at all, but now you are something else. You are the opposite of the extreme you didn't like. Now you are another extreme, but that doesn't work either. Conventional society fails to teach us how much our early conditioning affects us; it becomes part of our subconscious and we don't even see it. It stays within us and remains part of the invisible fabric of our thinking and our decision-making every single day.

Remembering the essence of our true selves, and the starting point we all shared and came from can help us as we try to eradicate obstacles that keep us from achieving our goals in life. We are pure spirit manifested into bodies. We are not solely bodies and mass, lumbering through life, waiting for life to happen to us. Each of us is designed as an auto-poetic being. We are in fact creators, with Universal Power readily accessible to us through our subconscious mind. We have the capacity, through our thoughts, to create every minute of our reality, and yet so many of us don't know this, don't believe this, or don't know how to fully implement this. I want you to learn how to tap into this potential, to your inherent creative potential.

For all of us, our minds never really stood a chance. For centuries our ancestors have passed down their thought patterns and beliefs, imprinting beliefs both positive and negative on each subsequent generation. Even your parents did not fully know what they were doing when they imprinted upon you all of the programming that you integrated from birth. They were just doing the best they could with what they knew. Often our parents were themselves repeating the conditioning that they experienced in their own families.

There may be no preventing this programming or imprinting; however, as adults, you can reverse the programming by using world-class subconscious mind programming techniques, such as those that are outlined in this book. Once you are aware of how much your subconscious impacts your conscious mind, you will seek out ways to overcome these thoughts, the ones you never chose, could not have chosen, and, really, had been chosen on your behalf. These techniques help you to separate yourself from the emotion, which is really what makes the thought real to your subconscious mind. These strategies, in effect, will help you erase and re-paint your canvas, so that the memory and content remain, while the emotion dissipates. The subconscious mind responds to visuals and emotion, and by disconnecting the emotion from the thought, we can move forward into changing certain areas of our lives that may once have been limited by these thoughts and the strong emotions they generated.

While it is impossible to revisit the blank canvas our minds once were in our lives, it is possible to reverse the damaging effects of all the negative thoughts that filled that canvas. It is possible to reprogram the subconscious mind, and it is possible to grow your intuition so you can truly see the divine connection within, the connection to all of creation. The techniques and methods in this book will show you how.

Chapter Three: Inside the Vault

Every day, in virtually everything we do, there exists the internal/external dichotomy. Things truly are never what they seem. Rarely do we get access to the deeper workings of the person, event, place, or activity we are with, engaging in, or taking part in. We tend to hang out on a very superficial plane of existence the majority of the time, focusing on how we look, judging others by how they look, and focusing on our physical bodies but not our true selves, the parts on the inside that feel and think. For some people, they may not even know that they are in possession of all of the innate wisdom of the universe in their minds. So many people barely use a fraction of their brain power, and still others will live their whole lives completely unaware of the power they have had all along; power that is inherent within the subconscious mind. Remember, the subconscious mind connects to the expression of Universal Power.

Just like when you go into a bank and see the desks, chairs, and bank tellers when you enter, but you do not see the vault where the money is hidden, so it is with our own vault. People see each other on a physical level, and see themselves on a physical level, and don't look deeper into the vault of others, or their own vault—in this case, the subconscious mind. What's worse is that so many people don't even know this vault exists! When you go to a bank, you are aware that what you are seeing is not the money or the gold; you know that the money and the gold exist in a special vault that is accessed in a specific way by specific people. It's time to think of your subconscious mind as that same kind of special vault, and only you can access it. In that vault is stored a treasure trove of freedom, wealth, good health, great relationships—you name it, you can access it in your vault. The subconscious mind contains access to everything you need—everything you need to be healthy, to be happy, to be wealthy, and to have the things you want in life. Most people don't even know about the existence of the subconscious mind, not to mention the power it contains.

Your vault is your subconscious mind, and it is where you are connected to Universal Power. Your subconscious mind is full of more wisdom, connection, and knowledge than you can even begin to fathom. While everyone sees the external you, your version of the nice chairs and desks and bank tellers, the power that is inside your vault is what is driving this external you. It is vital to first of all understand that you have unlimited power within you to create the life of your dreams, and second of all to understand that regardless of whether or not you know this, whatever is inside your vault has already been driving the external you. Wouldn't you like to switch places and get behind the steering wheel for a change?

The vault of your subconscious mind is full of potential. The subconscious mind is the seat of Universal Power. We are connected to all the knowledge in the universe through our subconscious mind. We are beings of creation and all we really want to do is create and expand, much like the universe that we are a part of does inherently. We cannot do this if we are constantly disregarding our dreams, intuitions, gut feelings, or callings and instead spending all our days wrapped up in intellectualizing everything we do. I am not saying you must get spiritual and activate your pineal gland or even meditate daily. You don't need to believe in God, even. But believing that there is a higher power in the universe and that you are one with that higher power through your subconscious mind can be helpful when you start getting serious about getting rid of fears, doubts, limiting thoughts, and long-running programs. It is this sense of connection to a larger existence that can remind us of our healthy place in the rich context of all things. We are all connected to that Ocean of Universal Power!

Further to what we agreed the subconscious mind to be in chapter one, another analogy I like to use when talking about the subconscious mind is to liken the subconscious as the hard drive to the computer that is your conscious mind. The subconscious stores all kinds of information that otherwise clutters up the conscious mind. The conscious mind is the source of logic, reason, and rational thought. Anything that you take in that cannot be processed by the conscious mind is integrated in the subconscious mind. This includes traumatic experiences, visual images, and virtually all information taken in through the senses. The subconscious mind stores this information, to be used in your life at any time, or to present itself to you when the need arises. Often, the subconscious mind will use the information it has stored to warn you, or trigger you, or sometimes it will bring this information to your attention, even when you have no idea what the connection or need might be behind it. Remember, the subconscious mind wants to protect you; it wants you to survive your life experiences.

The subconscious mind also controls all the functions of the body, as I elaborated on in chapter one. Take a deep breath right now. How you take this breath when you are using your conscious mind is very different from just breathing. Your subconscious mind plays a part in keeping you breathing without thinking about it, all day long. When you are sleeping, the subconscious keeps you breathing. Now, sitting still, accelerate your heart rate. Go ahead— accelerate your heart rate. Were you able to do it? Chances are you weren't. This is because you are hearing the request and responding to it on a conscious level. You cannot consciously direct your subconscious to alter the way your body is functioning. However, if you dream you are being chased by a tiger, your heart rate will go up, you'll start to sweat, perhaps even awaken in the middle of the night. These bodily functions were activated by the subconscious in response to the images your dreaming mind presented to it. The subconscious keeps you functioning and safe on the physical level.

Another example: If you eat a poisonous food, your subconscious mind is what leads the physical response to throw the poisonous food up so it doesn't stay in your body. There are all kinds of examples of the subconscious mind taking information and letting us perform activities without having to think about them. Driving a car is a great one— when you first learned to drive a car, you were likely very conscious of how to put your foot on the brake or the clutch, how to hold the steering wheel, how to shift gears. Think about how you drive your car now, however. Sometimes I will be halfway out of the driveway before I even need to bring my conscious attention to what I am doing! After so many years of driving, my subconscious mind has learned all of the moves and actions so that I can get into my car, put the key in the ignition and get driving without consciously having to think about any of the actions involved. This is like those habit patterns formed from early conditioning I mentioned earlier. Think about it—we drive and talk to people, we drive and fiddle with the stereo, we drive and eat! All that time, we are consciously talking to people, changing the music, or eating—which means that the information about driving stored in our subconscious mind is what is actually letting the driving happen.

The subconscious mind is the conduit to Universal Power, and is a reminder that you are made up of this Universal Power. The subconscious mind wants to manifest outwardly everything that it receives from you inwardly. That is to say, what you think will be expressed; this is part of the mandate of the subconscious. The subconscious mind, backed by Universal Power, and the nature of the universe as creation, just wants to create for you that which you desire. Which is why it is essential to be aware of your thoughts and choose to think in ways that attract to you what it is you want. Imagine knowing you have access to Universal Power (and Universal Power is really what drives the universe as the ultimate creator), backing you up as you strive to achieve your goals in life! My world-class subconscious mind programming techniques can help you get to this knowing—and get to a place where you make an ally of your subconscious mind.

We discussed in chapter two the idea that we are born with a blank canvas that is quickly imprinted with all the thoughts, fears, and beliefs of the influential figures around us as we grew up. Using subconscious mind programming techniques allows you to step out of the imprint on an emotional level so that you can no longer be held back by all of the clutter that has built up throughout your life in your subconscious mind. While you may never really empty the hard drive that is the subconscious mind, you can disable the power of the emotion connected to all that is stored within it. What I am saying is that you can't change your earlier experiences, but you can alter the way you relate to them. A strong emotion is what you are responding to when you are self-sabotaging, or old patterns resurface, or even unexplained fears or reactions to things take hold. If you have found yourself feeling anxious without really knowing why, or have fears that you can't understand why you have them, this is because the subconscious has a memory of an event and it is hanging on to this memory, and the original emotion that developed with it. The subconscious mind may be triggered by something in your conscious present that invokes the emotion of the event, even if you never knew or don't remember what that event is, you will feel this feeling and it could seriously hinder your life if it comes at the wrong time.

This part of the mind is truly locked away and very few people even know to access it in their lives, much less *how* to access it. Accessing your vault allows you to see what is stored there, and then clear the aspects that are no longer serving you. With this clearing, the vault can be unlocked, allowing you to access Universal Power and your own limitless potential. The subconscious mind is available to help maintain your body in good health. The subconscious mind is ready to help you become a millionaire by drawing money to you. The subconscious mind is ready to help you navigate your relationships so they become excellent relationships. The subconscious mind wants you to be an aligned human being so you can best serve the people around you and fulfill your mission as a part of creation in the universe. The subconscious mind is the universe working through you as a human. Are you starting to feel just how important the subconscious is—and how essential it is to have as an ally?

All you need to do is to unlock the subconscious mind—unlock your vault, as it were. The subconscious mind programming techniques—of which I will outline a few in subsequent chapters—were designed through my years of working in personal development as ways to help you unlock the vault so you can really get into the riches that are stored in it. These techniques are designed to take a look at what is in there, and then get to work on eradicating the emotion that limits you.

The subconscious mind is the most powerful part of our existence as humans. It really is our own vault where the real gold and riches are stored. Grasping the depth of potential that every human has inside of them is essential for moving forward into your life masterpiece. There is no need to fix anything, there is no need to add anything, you have all the answers that you seek; you just need a push in the right direction. That direction is reprogramming the subconscious, and I can show you how. If you knew that you had the power all along within you, would you not want to know how to access it to make your life better in every way imaginable? To align your life so that everything runs smoothly, from good health and financial success to great relationships and a sense of peace and well-being? This is what reprogramming your subconscious mind can do for you.

Chapter Four: Internal Influence

Your vault—that is, the subconscious mind—stores a wealth of information for you. All of your experiences, emotions, memories, things you have learned, things you have heard, things your parents told you, messages from the media, and messages from society. It's like an endless movie reel of data and information. All of this is in your subconscious mind and is therefore capable of influencing you in subtle and large ways. What is influencing you internally, or what I call your "internal influence," is impacting you more profoundly than you realize. The internal affects the external, so you can directly see the impact of your internal influence through what is happening to you and around you. Your internal influence is something to learn to be aware of—changing this will surely change what comes to you in your external environment.

There is one person you are with your whole life and that is you. Wherever you go, there you are. You are always with yourself. Keeping this in mind, are you aware of how you think? Have you noticed how you talk to yourself? Have you noticed how you react when you make a mistake, or things don't go your way? The tendency is to blame ourselves, or get mad at ourselves when we make mistakes. Of course, some people project the blame onto others, but don't be fooled—they are still blaming themselves. Many of these tendencies and cues have been gathered throughout the course of your life via your subconscious mind. Your inner 'movie reel' collected all of your life experiences and all of those messages and then designed a script that runs in your head. This script is married to that sense of safety and predictability that we talked about earlier. It repeats information that it thinks will help you maintain a known identity, so that you do not have to experience stepping out into an unknown identity. Have you ever wanted to step outside of yourself completely? Have you accepted that this is not possible? Of course it's not possible to disengage from yourself completely. However, what *is* possible is that you can change this internal script! You can reprogram the thoughts and ideas you loop internally to deeply affect life in every way imaginable! You, along with everyone else on the planet, have access to this magical portal. Yes, that's right, it's your subconscious.

This is neither about loving yourself, nor is it about ceasing to hate yourself. This is, however, about recognizing how you affect your behavior through your thoughts and beliefs and getting present to the fact that you do. The more you gain awareness of your conscious thoughts, the more you can rearrange those thoughts to be positive and affirming, signaling the same to your subconscious. This puts you on the path to becoming an ally to yourself instead of continuing to be your own adversary. If you are struggling and life is always miserable for you, take a look at your thoughts and you will find the root of your struggle. If you think you can't change your thoughts, think again. The choice between remaining a victim of limiting thoughts and beliefs or freeing yourself from these limiting thoughts and beliefs actually exists, and it's yours to be made. You are responsible for your internal environment, and therefore your external environment. Your internal environment greatly affects your life circumstances. In fact, your willingness and ability to relate, connect to, and design your interior life, by getting to know your own mind, is critical to changing your life circumstances. The trick is to learn how to get your subconscious on board and how to build and maintain that sturdy bridge between your conscious and subconscious minds, with you as the director shifting in the direction of your dream life.

Despite all of the Universal Power accessible to us through the subconscious mind, it remains that the subconscious mind still contributes to holding us back. For in that storehouse of all our experiences are also found all the patterns and beliefs that were given to us without our choosing them. I'm talking about all of the experiences you've had over the course of your lifetime. The subconscious mind, just like a sponge, has absorbed all of them. Whether from traumatic experiences during childhood or the programming from authority figures in your life, the majority of beliefs and patterns running from your subconscious were most definitely not chosen by you. What you can choose, however, is what thoughts are entering your conscious mind. You can become the discerning bouncer of the nightclub of your mind. The subconscious mind wants to make manifest that which the conscious mind is thinking, so the faster you get this concept and start working hard to armor your conscious mind with positive thoughts, the more you will be able to attract and create that which you desire.

It is important to distinguish who you really are in all of this. Are you your subconscious mind? Are you your conscious mind? Are you your identity (which was created out of your past and survival programming)? Are you your ego?

The ego is created from the first memories and events of your conscious mind. It is thus created from the outset, and, also from the outset, the ego created a barrier between you and the innate wisdom stored within the subconscious mind. Your ego rooted and solidified as your life wore on, and your patterns manifested as expected. You developed a set of characteristics and qualities that corresponded with your ego. This is mostly because you probably knew nothing else as you grew up, other than to perpetuate the patterns absorbed by the subconscious mind throughout your childhood. These patterns and programs are filled with defense strategies that are generated automatically whenever there is a threat to our identity. The ego is attached to the identity, commonly known as ego-identity, which makes the ego also not the full picture of who you really are. This is because you are not your identity! And you are not your ego. And you are not your ego-identity.

Contrary to popular belief, the voice in your head is also not you. The voice in your head is only a part of you. All the voice in your head knows it sees through the filter of the programming in your subconscious mind. We tend to trust the voice in our heads immensely, but it is not the seat of true wisdom for any of us. The voice in our head, what I will call ego, operates on the plane of logic and rational thinking, but is unable to access the more creative and wise aspects of the subconscious mind. The ego is a mechanism devised to help you survive through life on the physical plane. Much of our ego is constructed around a set of beliefs and ideas that are a direct result of our conditioning and our experiences. These, as we know, are formed largely as a result of external information and cues from those around us. The ego helps you interact with people and your experiences, like a mental point of reference or template. The ego also keeps the myth of separation alive for all of us. It tries to convince us that we are not all part of the universal ocean of oneness. The ego likes words like 'me' and 'mine' and it filters your experience through the smallest universe possible, the universe of 'me.'

Without being able to separate ourselves from our egos, we will never truly be able to see that we are entirely one with the universe. The ego is tenacious! It is as though it has a vested interest in convincing us that we do not have access to that infinite Universal Power that each of us does. How do we separate our sense of selves from our ego? Yes, you guessed it—by cultivating self-awareness. As we identify and recognize those underlying messages that come from our conditioning, we can begin to see that they are not actually who we are. You can relate to the ego as a necessary "cloak" of identity that enables you to be in relationship with yourself and with others, but never mistake it for your true *essence.* Through developing self-awareness, becoming aware of your own thoughts, patterns, and habits, and then actively choosing to replace the old programming with newer supportive information, you can shift your relationship to your own ego. You remove the ego from the driver's seat! By doing this, we put our connection to

Universal Power, our sense of ourselves as omnipotent, in front of the wheel. When we take the ego out of the driver's seat, we give ourselves the opportunity to build a stronger connection to our subconscious mind, that limitless vault of Universal Power.

Tangled up in our manufactured identities and the surviving ego is our self-esteem. We often seek help improving our self-esteem and self-image by reading books, or turning to programs developed and run by experts in personal development. What I have learned in my years of personal development work is that the only way to improve self-esteem and self-image in a deeper, more integrated way is by turning to world-class subconscious reprogramming techniques. We must connect to and rewire our subconscious mind in order to create a new foundation for our lives. This is the seat of our access to change and our ability to shift the course of our lives. There is no self-help book in the world that you can just read that will suddenly give you high self-esteem. You have to practice and implement the techniques daily, regardless of the book, program, or teacher, in order to affect change. When you choose to work with your subconscious mind, however, you will get more effective results much faster. It's like choosing to fuel your car with the highest octane, purest source of gas versus going for the usual, run-of-the-mill unleaded variety. Sustainable, potent, and rapid change comes from choosing and committing to work directly with your subconscious. When you do this, your life course changes rapidly and with more ease. Simple, effective, world-class tools and techniques will be revealed to you so that you can begin to chart the course of your life according to your wishes and dreams!

Having a healthy self-esteem begins in your childhood. Self-esteem is about how we value ourselves. It determines how we perceive our value to the world and how valuable we think we are to others. Self-esteem affects so many parts of our lives including our trust in others, our relationships, our work—virtually every part of our lives is impacted by how we bring ourselves to each interaction. Self-esteem is a core part of the mechanism that directly influences our sense of belonging, and how we relate to others. Self-esteem is directly connected to our sense of self-respect and self-satisfaction, and is expressed as having a sense of confidence. There is a spectrum of self-esteem states, and we can shift between them, from one to another. Positive self-esteem gives us the strength and flexibility to be the ones in charge of our lives. Positive self-esteem supports our ability to grow and our capacity for resilience, and enables us to move beyond fear of rejection and view mistakes as opportunities for growth.

On the other side of the spectrum is poor or low self-esteem. Authority figures in our lives—parents, teachers, and bosses—have a huge impact on how our self-esteem developed. If you were raised with parents who neglected you, boom! There goes your self-esteem. If you were raised with parents who doted on you, boom! There goes your self-esteem in the opposite direction. If you had the parent of the opposite sex treat you differently in any way, this can affect your self-esteem. Particularly if you are a woman and your father did not help you cultivate your self-image, your self-esteem may not have risen to the level it should be. If you went to school and your teachers made a comment that you were not smart, boom! There goes your self-esteem.

Sometimes the example of a balloon is used to illustrate our self-esteem. When we receive excessive praise or admiration for work that we have done, our self-esteem can overinflate, like a balloon with too much air or helium inside. People with excessive self-esteem can become boastful or smug, sometimes trying to convince others of their own superiority. When we take in excessive criticism or hurtful comments about our work or behavior, we can develop poor self-esteem, like a deflated balloon. Having poor self-esteem can make us feel as though we don't have value in the world and that the work we do doesn't matter. Sometimes this can lead to self-destructive or self-defeating behaviors. No matter what the interaction, big or small, your emotional reaction at the time of the experience would have been felt by the subconscious mind and the memory of this is still held in your vault. These memories contributed to you having a healthy balanced self-esteem, an excessively high self-esteem, or a poor or low self-esteem. Each of these conditions has an immense impact on how we perceive ourselves in the world, influencing our sense of value or sense of worthlessness. What can you do about this? First, as I've mentioned previously, you must determine where your self-esteem is on the self-esteem spectrum. Then, decide to change your self-esteem back to a higher, but balanced place. How? You reprogram your subconscious mind, giving you access to the memory that initially helped to create your self-esteem, and then, by separating out the emotion that was initially attached to the experience. You want to be able to have the memory, but to have it in a more neutral way, without so much emotion 'clouding' your memory of the experience. When you remove the emotion from the experience, you give yourself the opportunity for a new perspective of who you are, thus enabling you to directly increase your self-esteem.

Why is good self-esteem important, anyway? I know, it's a rhetorical question. Self-esteem is directly related to our internal set of expectations about ourselves. Good self-esteem is what will get you to take action in your life—and you only get results by taking action. I mean it when I say that there is absolutely no use for low self-esteem. Low self-esteem serves to keep you stuck in limiting patterns and perpetuates the victim mentality. Low self-esteem keeps you stuck in the mailroom when you belong in the corner office with big windows. Low self-esteem keeps you single when you know you have a lot of love to give and deserve a healthy relationship. It serves no one—and you serve no one—when you are indulging in it. And yes, it is actually indulgent to wallow in a perpetual sense of self-esteem!

That's right—I said it is indulgent to be stuck in low self-esteem. This is because ultimately, like anything, low self-esteem is a choice. If you suffer from low self-esteem, although you certainly did not choose to be imprinted with it or grow up with the experiences you had that created it, you are in your present life also not choosing to overcome it. This is how it limits you. If you really understand that you can choose to have high self-esteem, that having low self-esteem is not a curse or something you cannot erase and undo, then you can do the work you need to do to raise your self-esteem. Low self-esteem is not part of your DNA! When you consider the true nature of who you are, as something that emerged from Universal Power and is connected to Universal Power, the very notion of self-esteem at all is entirely ridiculous! I'm offering but one channel for you to explore when seeking to raise your self-esteem—there are many. I know that subconscious mind reprogramming is the most effective because it cuts right to the core of the emotion behind the cause. You can set yourself free and be your own best friend just by raising your self-esteem. It is that simple. The techniques and methods in this book will show you how to do this.

Let's illustrate the two main expressions of self-esteem using an example. Let's say there is a set of twins, Sam and Shelley. When the twins were nine, their parents divorced and Sam went to live with his mother, Karen, and Shelley went to live with her father, Hank. Karen was a successful life insurance sales broker, breaking sales records many years in a row. She was raised in a loving family and had great relationships with her family and friends. Karen remained single for a couple of years following her divorce from Sam and Shelley's dad. Everyone who ran into her remarked on her poise, grace, friendliness, and sense of confidence. Shelley loved being a parent and she and Sam had a great relationship, even into Sam's early teenage years. Sam was successful at school, held a part-time job, and even ran for school president.

Hank married his mistress as soon as his divorce with Sam and Shelley's mom went through. Hank's new wife,

Roberta was much younger than Karen. At first, Shelley really liked living with her dad. He paid a lot of attention to her, praised her academic achievements and her success on sports teams, and devoted time to parenting her to the best of his ability. As Shelley moved into her teenage years, Hank began to spend all of his time with Roberta and his job and completely neglected his role as a doting father. At the same time, her grades began to slip, she quit her sports teams, and she began having one boyfriend after another, not spending much time with her girlfriends. When Shelley began to fail a couple of her classes, her guidance counselor called her in to talk to her about her grades and her truancy, and eventually they got to the topic of her self-esteem. In talking with the school counselor, Shelley discovered that she had very low self-esteem and that this was contributing to her difficulty in school, her difficulty in her social circles, and her lack of enthusiasm for the sports teams she used to love. When her father turned his full attention onto his new wife, Shelley's self-esteem plummeted. She tried to counter this loss of investment by her father through having relationships with boyfriends. Once Shelley and her counselor became aware of the origin of some of her poor self-esteem, she was sent back to the guidance counselor to address it. Shelley worked with the guidance counselor to understand how her mind had developed feelings of inadequacy through experiencing her father's neglect. Shelley's counselor helped Shelley to understand that she had allowed her own mind to turn against herself, thus eroding her capacity for success at school, in her social circles and, most importantly, her sense of place and value in the world. Shelley's counselor explained to her that she could actually reprogram her mind with more supportive and empowering thoughts, feelings, and ideas, so that she could replace the limiting beliefs with ones that nourished her success. She explained to Shelley that she could, in fact, become her own best friend.

Why wouldn't you want to be your own best friend? You are with yourself 24/7, 365! Imagine if, instead of being angry with yourself for running late all the time, you had nothing but acceptance and compassion for yourself? Chances are, with acceptance and compassion for yourself, you would eventually turn your late behavior into punctuality. What if, instead of being hard on yourself for eating that donut, you just ate the donut and were happy about it? Chances are the donut will process much more easily through your digestive system—and you will be less likely to reach for a second one. I'm not even asking you to love yourself—although it's pretty close! You can fake it until you make it, as they say, when it comes to growing your self-esteem. If you have to look in the mirror daily and tell yourself how awesome you are, then so be it. You could also reprogram your subconscious mind and replace days and months and years of repeating positive affirmations with one session using the right tools and techniques—like the ones we'll discuss in chapter eleven.

When you switch your internal influence paradigm from being one where you constantly belittle yourself to one where you are your own cheerleader, you will see the benefits immediately. It is a total waste of time to remain in low self-esteem, especially because there are effective methods for raising it. Low self-esteem may serve you because chances are it keeps you out of trouble, keeps you comfortable, and perhaps even keeps you feeling safe. It may feel comfortable to remain in a place of low self-esteem because the thought of change creates a strong sense of fear for you. If you have low self-esteem and let it keep you from taking action, then guess what? You are avoiding your life! Staying in low self-esteem lets you be complacent, it absolves you of responsibility and it helps you avoid fear. You take no risks when you take no action. You don't grow, you don't move yourself forward and you don't challenge yourself to keep improving. You become like water that has become stagnant, and we all know what stagnant water smells like!

Low self-esteem is a self-perpetuating state of being, and until you actively seek to overcome it, you will be living a life that is completely cut off from achieving what you want, paralyzed by low self-esteem. Further, you will constantly be wallowing in a state of self-hate, and then you will find that you are no fun to be with—and here you are, stuck with yourself all the time. Think about what keeps you in low self-esteem. Take a good look around you at everyone else and see who is taking action and who isn't. Some of those doers don't even have high self-esteem—yet. But the very fact of their willingness to take action is leading them in the right direction. Take a step in the direction of raising your self-esteem and you will see how the universe will rise up to show you how big you can really go. Everything you want in the world—including a new and improved you—is waiting for you to activate it by clearing your subconscious mind and establishing positive thoughts in your conscious mind. This directly influences your self-esteem, your expectations, and subsequently the actions you take in the world.

If low self-esteem is an unhelpful way to be, what is high self-esteem then? When you become your own best friend, you pave the way for other people to love and accept themselves. You act from an empowered place, in alignment with your internal values. You are also more willing to take action to make things happen in your life. You are much less narcissistic than when you have low self-esteem. Believe it! All that time caught up in thinking you're worthless is really vain! People with high self-esteem want to serve others. They know that giving makes them feel good. They are going for their goals with love. They have a zest for life that is palpable. It's up to you which side you want to be on, but it is the people with high self-esteem that make things happen in the world. High self-esteem is such an important part of the process of developing your potential, of becoming the fullest expression of yourself!

It is not worth blaming your past, your parents, or whomever it might be that you hold responsible for having low self-esteem. It is, however, worth doing some personal work to increase your self-esteem so you can transcend all the negative and limiting stories you have been hanging on to and step into what you are really capable of in the world. Reprogramming your subconscious mind is a fast and effective way to get there, let me assure you. Your ability to influence yourself internally is huge; in fact, it's all there is. So it is vital that you get your internal influence aligned in a way that will serve you and your highest self and vision for your life. Your internal dialogue becomes the story you tell yourself every day—this is the voice that witnesses and reflects to you your perceptions of everything that happens to you in a day. This is your inner world, which translates directly into your outer world. This is where your power emanates from, and so many people nowadays don't grasp this concept. In the West, we live in a world that is constantly bombarding us with media, sounds, and images, along with a whole multitude of external distractions. To take the time to become aware, to tune in to and work with your subconscious mind effectively is the most powerful tool available to you. This is the only way you can change the course of your life and bring your goals into your reality.

So many people don't know this or don't see this and give away their power to others constantly. But your internal influence is your power, and you must learn to recognize and utilize your power to bring you all the good in the world that you desire. Begin to believe that you do hold that power within yourself! Stop playing small and keeping yourself out of the game! Grow your self-esteem, take risks and step into living large! Let me show you the steps and methods that will move you in this direction.

The only thing holding you back in this life is you. There is no better time than right now to choose to become your own best friend and cheerleader and influence yourself from the inside out in the most positive way possible.

Chapter Five: Mental Intimacy

Throughout the ages, thinkers, artists, spiritual teachers and many others have contemplated what it is to be human. Despite the story of separation that has a stronghold on how we believe it is to be human, there is in fact another idea about the human condition. This idea has been mentioned in countless religions, ancient teachings, and cultures—even religions that war with one another throughout the ages. This idea is that, rather than being separate from all of nature/the Universe/God, we are, in fact, all connected. At the core of this concept is the idea that we are all universal consciousness. Whatever you choose to call it—God, the Universe, Spirit, Great Mystery—it is present within you. I call it Universal Power, and it's part of your DNA, inside every single cell.

Universal Power is also accessed through your subconscious mind, and this is true of every human on earth. Spiritual teachers and scientists alike have realized that our thoughts create our realities, and this is because of our connection to Universal Power. Universal Power is all-knowing, creative, and intelligent. Another word for it is "source," and its entire mission is to create and keep expanding upon itself. Its mission is growth and expansion and you are part of this mission! All of the laws of the universe have this irrefutable truth as the backbone. The Law of Attraction, for instance, that says that like attracts like, is entirely evidence to the fact that what we think becomes reality. Where do our thoughts come from? We generate our thoughts in the conscious mind. The subconscious mind awaits the thoughts, ready to create—because it is the conduit to Universal Power, and Universal Power is creation itself.

The real truth to grasp is that you are IT. You are God, the universe, source, all of creation. If you truly want to fulfill your destiny as a human being, as a part of Universal Power, you will recognize that you are here to create, and you will also see that you *do* create your life in every moment. What most people fail to understand is the power of this in their day-to-day lives. It is not just self-help talk to suggest you do affirmations and visualizations and you will get what you want. It is not just woo-woo or overly spiritual to say you are the source and the universe. Everything is connected, everything is energy, every thought you think yields a result, and every idea you have comes to you from this greater knowing beyond yourself, Universal Power. Remember, Universal Power is built into your DNA! The subconscious mind is the keeper of this access to Universal Power, and regardless of whether or not you choose to believe it, this is the truth of seekers and scientists throughout the ages. There is a greater intelligence at work, and it works through us, through our subconscious minds. This is the portal to the omnipotent and infinite life-source that connects all things in the Universe.

Everything that has been created in life has come from this Universal Power, channeled through humans who understood this truth and allowed it to come through. We don't have to accept a life of lack or poverty, or even a life of non-creativity once we fully integrate this knowledge. We have the power to manifest everything we dream of, if we recognize this and do some work to release limiting beliefs and practice some of the techniques I will share with you. The ideas that came through Edison, Einstein, Oprah, Steve Jobs, Martha Stewart, or Bill Gates came out of the same Universal Power that creates trees, animals, all the life in the ocean, and, indeed, life as we know it. We are creation, and we can either create lack, disappointment, and failure in our lives, or create lives that contribute to our fellow humans, and create wealth and happiness for ourselves *and* others.

Let's go back to the concept of ideas for a moment here. Indeed, one of the most fascinating parts of your mind are ideas. Where do they come from? How are they sourced? What is their origin? What's their catalyst to come into being? What is their genesis? What is an idea? Is it something that takes all the known physical sense that combines them into a thought? Or is an idea indeed something more? Above, I alluded to the fact that ideas generate out of Universal Power. Actually, ideas are the actual fruition of conduits to other energy sources that are out there.

Even people who do not believe in higher mind learning will still subscribe to the fact that an idea is not a physically generated form. Thus, it is energetic—and the more we reveal its energetic nature, the more it fits that it is a byproduct of creation, the Universe as creation, and human beings as a part of that creation.

An idea is actually an evolutionary function of the mind's activity. It is a moving forward to where you're actually creating a thought process that is not based necessarily on physical stimuli but on mental or energetic stimuli. It's beyond values that are idealized by the subconscious mind, which always has a need for expression. Ideas are the form of that expression.

The subconscious mind is not sedentary, it is active 24/7, 365 and it is in a constant state of need for expression. It draws from our physical experiences and our storage banks, because the subconscious never forgets anything. These creative ideas are the result of the evolution of the thought processes, so they engage and guarantee a constant activity of the mind and allow the mind to remain in its non-sedentary state. Ideas do not correspond to any type of finality, although they express forcefully many times because they are repetitive in nature. The stronger the emotionalized thought, the more it will cast a broader web in order to bring an idea into your mind.

It is important to note that the idea does not actually come from man himself. Rather, it will pulse through you as an accumulation of thought processes, both your own and those of energies that you're exposed to. It then combines with the physical nature of what your thought processes and dominant thoughts are, and then comes to fruition as an idea or a concept. Now, if it is not emotionalized to a level to where it engages at a deep psychic level, then the idea may be a fleeting idea.

How many times have we had an idea that haunts us over and over and over, and it seems as if that's all we can think about? Why is that? Why the repetitive nature? It's not necessarily Obsessive-Compulsive Disorder; it is simply an idea that is expressing itself. It is formed in energetic form in the mind and is now expressing itself through your mind and then ultimately through the physical manifestation of that idea.

Everything you look at began as a thought. The table you are sitting at, the chair you are sitting on, the car you are driving, the pencil you are holding, the phone you are listening to, they all became an idea first, and then became a tangible item. Ideas are really the functional genesis of the entire physical world that we live in. So if we regress back to when there were no items in our world, when there were no cars or chairs or clothing or anything else, then we would regress all the way back to pure energy. We would have to, because what is the precursor of an item? A thought, and thoughts are energy.

Therefore, before there were items, there could only be pure energy. Then that pure energy became an idea that took shape in the form of an item.

So if this is indeed the case, then is it not true that thought or energy can create? It is absolutely true! This is true because the creation is the accumulation of the dominant thought. If, for instance, you wanted something bad enough, like Steve Jobs wanted to make an excellent computer way back when he began, and it seemed to be non-existent, the universe would have the ability to create that for you. Contrary to the Law of Attraction, however, the universe will not bring it to you, literally. You can program and pray on the love of your life and she or he won't just appear in a puff of smoke. He or she will, however, manifest in the form of circumstance. This is because an energetic footprint has now been made on universal energy, and then synchronized with the origin which is you.

The energy footprint on the universe was synchronized by the initial thought you put out there, and the creative process went to work. Knowing and understanding this, you then see why it is imperative that we learn to control our thoughts, and listen to ideas.

If we move back to way before our physical reality, and see that the origin is pure energy, is it not true that we could utilize this origin to create again? If it can be done once, it can be done twice. People that understand this process are able to create by design incredible lives. Some people think it's the "Midas touch," or they get lucky, but it's actually because they're in a constant state of self-creation, energizing footprints on universal energy, whose origin is their own energy in the form of an idea which is dormant seeking expression. It is the most profound concept, and when put to use in your life it will produce profound results.

Which is what happened to virtually all creators and inventors and people we know to be "great minds" throughout all time. However, before we take this truth and apply it to creating your life, let's look at who you really are—and assess how familiar you are with your true self.

In the simplest of terms, your being, or self, is made up of four core elements. You are a physical being, a mental being, an emotional being, and a spiritual being. Regardless of what your spiritual beliefs are, we can all agree that there needs to be a holistic harmony between all four parts of ourselves, because who and what we are, in essence, is the sum of these four parts. This sense of harmony is also referred to as alignment. It is important to be intimate in relationship with yourself, and by this I mean intimate and honest with the internal parts of yourself, your internal influence, as we discussed in the previous chapter. You need to know and understand the mechanics of your inner world before you can make changes that will influence your outer world.

To become intimately familiar with yourself is to become authentic. Being authentic means being genuinely truthful about who you are. When we are living in harmony with our inner values, we feel a stronger sense of authenticity. When we are living authentically, we are true to ourselves, and living according to our sense of inner truth. This is probably why the old saying, "Be yourself, no matter what they say!" has stuck around—it encourages us to live in the truth of who we are, our most authentic selves. Living authentically gives us permission to be 'real' and gives us a sense of freedom. When we live with authenticity, we are not pretending or lying or creating fantasies to please other people or the conventions of society. If any aspects of your life are out of alignment, you will not be congruent with your internal value system. If you are not living life congruently, you will not achieve your goals.

One of the most important strategies that I've used is called 'parts alignment.' Many of us have heard the expressions, a 'part' of us is nervous, a 'part' of us is scared, a 'part' of us is happy, a 'part' of us is sad. What 'part' exactly are you talking about? We're talking about a part of the mind. It is through that authenticity and self-transparency that you will allow yourself to become intimately familiar with your own mind. It is a place that can be scary for many people, because harbored within our minds are our fears. We use a form of self-deception to move away from our fears, not unlike somebody covering their eyes when they feel that they are scared or are about to be hurt. They will cover their eyes because it's an unconscious movement not to see the threat. In this same way, we cover the eyes of our minds on many occasions. We prefer not to feel or engage or experience the threat or the perception. By moving away, we are actually not being transparent with ourselves. The more transparent you are with yourself, then the more you're able to ascertain what area it is that you need to address to improve yourself.

Think of it like a mental x-ray. If you were to close your eyes and not look at the x-ray, then you would be unable to pinpoint where you needed to put your attention. If you're doing a mental x-ray of your mind, your subconscious, then you know where you need to focus your attention to eliminate whatever is causing the discomfort in your mind, or, in a physical sense, whatever is causing discomfort in the body. Mental surgical intervention takes place when you remove yourself from self-deception and accept the reality that there are things that you've accumulated over the years that need to be addressed. There may be health issues that have built up that need to be addressed, whether it's arterial plaque, or friction on a joint. You're now going to become the care-taker of your own mind, just like you are the caretaker of your own health. When you have the ability to remove yourself from that deception and see with clarity, then you're able to move forward very quickly.

Many times we have a tendency to not want to hear criticism. Now that's a natural response for virtually everyone. No one likes the feeling of being criticized because we strive for approval. Criticism is not unlike coaching, and there are many different kinds. There is healthy or constructive criticism and there is demeaning criticism. Regardless of what it is, it is important that you accept the criticism as information only, with no emotional reaction or attachment to it. If it serves you, then address it just like an x-ray that someone gave you. If it doesn't serve you or it's not valid, then guess what, it's like an x-ray that was taken incorrectly. Consider the example of the x-ray as a way to help you locate an area in your life that needs your attention. In order to be transparent, you must be open to listening to life's lessons. Life lessons, learned through the day-to-day experiences, whether positive or challenging, give you a direction on where to go. It's no different than you looking up and seeing a thunderstorm and deciding not to take that flying course that day. Life's lessons come in the form of criticism. They come in the form of abandonment. They come in the form of competition. They come in the form of love. They come in the form of hatred, and so on, and so forth. There are many different types of life lessons that are like mental x-rays, allowing you to pinpoint exactly where the discomfort and the origin is. Once you've found the origin of the discomfort, you must move away from self-deception, and move towards self-authenticity and self-transparency. Self-authenticity and self-transparency are what the champions of the mind utilize on a daily basis. They want to know themselves in an honest way so they can re-craft how they will be in the world.

Here is an example of self-deception and inauthenticity in action. Imagine you have begun to practice yoga at a local studio. For all of your life, you have been eating meat and fish and you have felt healthy and fit, in part due to your eating choices. Over the course of several months, you begin to build community and connection with this yoga studio. One evening, you are invited to a potluck dinner at the yoga studio. You bring your Aunt's favorite recipe for apple-cranberry crisp. To your surprise, none of the food on the potluck table contains any meat. Later, you find yourself in conversation with one of your favorite yoga teachers. She is talking about the atrocities of eating meat and suggesting that people who eat meat have no compassion whatsoever. This hits you on the inside strongly! You have been enjoying the benefits of yoga and particularly this teacher's classes for quite some time. She turns to you and asks you what your usual diet is. You name off all kinds of your favorite recipes, but you do not include any of your meat dishes. Your teacher says to you, smiling, "Oh, I had a feeling you were a vegetarian." Instead of correcting her, you smile in agreement. Something inside you begins to gnaw uncomfortably. Some part of you realizes that saying that you are a vegetarian, to please your teacher, is not only inauthentic, it is entirely untrue! Do you see how easy it can be to say and do things that are incongruent with your inner value system? Can you empathize with the desire to seek approval from outside people, especially those in positions of authority, at the expense of your true self?

Even if you want to continue to live life as if you are only a physical being, eventually you will come face-to-face with the reality that we are energetic entities, and power is eternal. Living life purely from the physical element means we can only react to life in a physical manner. You can react mentally and emotionally too, but those outputs have limited abilities. Something has to be more powerful that can create an all-encompassing outcome that is beyond the physical and can also manifest.

You are a spiritual being that is a compilation of energy. As you become familiar with yourself, you strengthen your ability to interact with the energy of the greater good or purpose or entity. We often exhaust ourselves trying to accomplish things physically, mentally, or emotionally when the truth is that we can step back and release it all to the greater power around us. If you are Christian, you might say, "Let go and let God"; other spiritual people might say, "Turn it over to the universe." Regardless of the words you use, the idea is to get out of your own way, understand that you are part of universal consciousness, all is connected, you have everything you want already even if it isn't manifested in the physical realm, and all you have to do is be.

This ability to get out of your own way from the control aspect of the physical, mental, and emotional and turn your desires or requests over to the energetic or spiritual aspects is what will allow you to have peace within. This is the peace that will help you to manifest and progress along your own path.

When you emphasize control over the physical and emotional aspects of yourself, there are more limitations present. You find yourself controlling how you want life to go, which only leads you to being derailed when things don't go your way. Once you understand what you are, which is a being that operates within four planes—those being the physical, mental, emotional, and spiritual planes—you will understand that you are a part of Universal Power. Maybe you have heard the expression that we are 'spiritual' beings having a human experience? Call it 'God' or 'spirit' or 'the universe,' it is within you and it is your subconscious mind. The entire notion of being separate from one another is an illusion. The truth is, we are all connected, and everything we need and desire in the world is already present for us.

Once you become familiar with what you really are as a human, you can then release the control aspect and allow the energetic component to expand. This creates more trust, faith, and belief that you are always supported by the universe. This trust, faith, and belief is what is required to manifest that which you desire. Not only will this faith and belief allow you to truly see how your thoughts create your reality, but this will also allow you to deepen into your authentic experience of yourself. The more congruent you become, with all your 'parts' aligned, the more resilient you will be to criticism, of any kind. The more you become intimately familiar with your inner self on the mental plane, the more so much superfluous self-judgment dissipates and the easier it becomes to discern when you are acting from an inauthentic place. This is what I mean by mental intimacy. This is how to build on your relationship with yourself to improve your internal influence, and from here truly access the aid of the Universal Power via the subconscious mind.

Part 2: The Inside Becomes the Outside

Chapter Six: It's Not Where You Are, It's Where You're Going

When we realize we yearn for change in our lives, at the beginning it can feel like we will be forever trapped in who we were or used to be. Indeed, the past is highly influential in our present life, whether we are aware of it or not. Past experiences inform all kinds of decisions we make in a day, some of which we make without thinking. When you decide to enter into a new relationship with someone, your past experiences may make you wary or afraid of being hurt. When you create a new piece of music or a piece of art, past experiences of how your creativity has been received will inform how you go about presenting that piece. When you really want to start to make change, first you have to allow yourself to be free of the past. Consider: It's not where you are right now, but where you're going, and let this be among the primary motivators in getting you to take the necessary steps to change. This means looking forward, not looking back; looking forward to who you want to be, not looking only at who you are right in this moment. It is a fine line to dance on, but being able to see the potential of who you are and how it can evolve as you decide to change your life is what will get you to a place of achieving your goals and desires.

Let me share with you two of the most motivating emotional states for creating change and success. These are inspiration and desperation. Desperation can be a good thing because until you get really dissatisfied, you won't do anything to take your life to another level. Dissatisfaction, then, is actually awesome! And dissatisfaction is an opportunity to turn struggle into something else. If you are feeling completely satisfied, you will become comfortable. When we feel comfortable, we are unlikely to make changes in our lives. Then life begins to deteriorate.

After all, it is not what you accomplish in relation to others that is important, it's what you accomplish in relationship to your own potential. Your tomorrow is based on your today, and once you realize that the ability to create your brightest tomorrow is already within you, you will start moving in the best direction for yourself, the direction of change for the better. You will move into an empowered place in the course of your own life.

Your brain is the most powerful computer on the planet. When you learn to use it properly, you can create any result you want. Your brain can give you the answer to almost any problem you have. The problem is that this computer we call our brain is not user-friendly, and does not come with an owner's manual. This book will show you how to operate your supercomputer with precision. Lasting change is not created in your life by learning more. Lasting change is created by dissolving the emotions, thoughts, patterns, beliefs, and programming that simply no longer serve you, in order to allow yourself to truly tap into your connection with

Universal Power. You must re-design your blueprint to create the kind of results you want in your life.

This is the basis of the work I am inviting you to do with this book. Today, you are beginning a process that can truly change the quality of your life forever and can take that paint-by-numbers life you might be living now and create the masterpiece called your life. So just for a moment now, what I want you to do is imagine that your life is a painting. Imagine that you have died and are looking down at that painting. What did you leave behind? Is your life a masterpiece that is cherished and hangs prominently as an example for others of what is possible, or is it a paint-by-numbers life that is packed away in someone's basement?

Where you are in your life right now is the direct result of making decisions unconsciously, stuck in patterns and beliefs that served you once, but have not evolved to continue to serve you now, as an adult. If you feel stuck or are not pleased with your circumstances, being aware of the choices you make—choices that come from someplace other than your conscious thoughts—is step number one to taking control of your life. If you feel great about your life, you can also benefit from this work, as there are still doubtless limiting beliefs and thoughts in your subconscious mind that affect you too, whether you realize it or not.

It's not about where you are; it's about where you're going. If you want to change your life and align all major aspects of your life—finances, health, relationships, emotional well-being—then looking at what shaped you and stepping out of a limiting identity is what will help you to make the changes you seek. In other words, you must become the kind of person who holds and embodies the characteristics and qualities that you value. Visualizing it, affirming it, and even living your life by a new set of standards is not going to work long term until this stuff goes from your conscious to your subconscious and finally into your heart. Not only do you have to DO it, and not only do you have to LIVE it, you also have to BECOME it. Then, you will manifest it.

For us to really live consciously, to be an example for others, we have to be aware of what is shaping us. Be aware of what programs your subconscious mind is already running, be aware of how the conscious and subconscious mind work together, and be aware of the thoughts you think that are disempowering, and how you can change those thoughts to empowering ones.

It is always amazing to me how people take more time in a day to pick out what they are going to watch on television than on programming their minds. We spend more time choosing what kind of products we're going to use to clean our bodies than considering how we are going to clean our minds! We put so much emphasis on the external, when the reality is that the external is driven by the internal. If you want success in money, relationships, health, and emotional health, you must start to work from the inside out.

It all comes down to the power of your mind, and this includes both your conscious and subconscious mind. You have in your power the ability to transform your thoughts into your allies or your adversaries. You are creating you each day through the thoughts you think. The subconscious mind is a direct connection to Universal Power, or source, or whatever higher power there is for you. The subconscious mind responds to images and emotions that come to your mind through your thoughts. You have in your life exactly what you tell yourself you want; that is, if you are frustrated, you're telling yourself you're frustrated. If you're saying "I'm sick," then you are not enjoying good health. Our internal communication is the dialogue we have with ourselves each day, and it is mostly filled with old programming. This is how our subconscious minds work, without our even being aware of how they are working behind the scenes to sabotage us. Our internal communication perpetuates the realization of what we expect.

If your internal communication is laden with limiting beliefs, or running on patterns that have been held in your subconscious for your whole life, then you will not be able to live to your fullest potential. Your patterns of thought and beliefs that no longer serve you must be sacrificed if you want to align all elements of your life. When I say "It's not where you are, it's where you're going," this is what I'm talking about. Where you are right now, as you read this, continues to be the self that is held hostage by an identity formed when you were a child. You are being held hostage by the patterns your subconscious mind is running in the background of your every waking moment. Until you reprogram your subconscious mind to make conscious choices in place of these choices made out of habit, you will not be able to move yourself out of where you might feel stuck and into where you will prosper. I'm not just talking about prosper financially either! I'm talking about prospering in whatever area you want to prosper—health, relationships, emotional well-being, sure, finances too. The big picture "prosper" —another word for it is thrive. To move from surviving to thriving means moving forward into where you're going, and not staying settled into where you are.

Take stock of where you are right now, and start to see where you can bridge the gap between where you are, and where you want to go. Where you are going in your life depends upon the choices you make today. Picking up this book was one choice you made that can serve you as you step forward more fully into your life. Eating a donut mindlessly on your drive home from work was one choice that may have been completely unconscious, one that may have served your eight-year-old self, starving for love from your mother, but one that doesn't serve your vision of being fit and strong. (Note that, occasionally indulging in a donut is ok, but making it a habit or doing it without thinking is not supporting your health goals.) By setting the intention to change, and deciding to make choices with awareness, through building smart connection between the subconscious and conscious minds, moment to moment, you will have a direct impact on each tomorrow as you build the future that you seek.

A close and careful read of this book is a unique opportunity to look deep inside yourself. Take a good look inside of your relationships, your decisions about money, and your decisions about your career, your relationship with the universe, or your higher power, and even your body. You will begin to understand how your own upbringing has influenced you and start identifying some of the decisions and habits you have created, including pinpointing one core decision that has affected your identity. Get clear about what really stands in your way (hint: it's you!).

Shifting your focus to become the kind of person you want to be has everything to do with YOU. If you want to change any circumstance or any relationship in your life, then you must begin with yourself, no matter how convinced you are that something else or somebody else must change. This is where we begin to shift from blaming others for our circumstances and recognizing our own internal sense of agency and power in building and sustaining the life of our dreams. Recognizing the patterns and habits that keep you in a place of 'smallness' and fear is the first step. Then, as you begin to make shifts and changes, you will find yourself able to change even the most rigid system and stubborn person. I have experienced this myself. Every small change and shift is progress, and this moves you forward. Any movement forward, as a result of your desire and courage to make lasting changes creates the opportunity for every other part of your life to be moved forward as well. Everything is interrelated, especially the parts of our lives that comprise the whole of our lived existence.

The past may have a hold on your present; indeed, it is a tricky one to extricate yourself from. However, you don't need to let it sit in the driver's seat. Taking control of your life and keeping a clear eye on the path ahead is one way of stepping out of the entanglement of the past. Use what you have learned, of course, but leave all that which is unnecessary. They call it 'baggage' for a reason! Where you are right now is the starting point for where you're going. It is okay, nay, even necessary, to imagine yourself as who you want to be, and to let these imaginings trump any more carryover of feelings associated with who you were. It's not where you are, or were, but where you're going that matters when you begin the journey of reprogramming your subconscious mind.

Chapter Seven: Everyone dies, but not everyone lives

Are you truly aware of the preciousness of each moment in your life? Are you aware of the constant trickling of sand through your hourglass of life? Are you living each moment fully, playing the biggest game you can, achieving your goals, and using the time you have wisely?

Chances are you, like so many others in the world, are not truly aware of the preciousness of each minute. For many, it takes a big shake-up, like the death of a loved one, or contraction of a terminal illness, for them to realize life is short. After this kind of wake-up call, people re-consider how they spend their time. Sadly, it is all too common that people procrastinate and postpone their life, and let that be the guiding paradigm for how they live. If you are one of these people, let me ask you—how is this working for you? How does the procrastination serve you? Have you written your bestseller yet? Made a million dollars? Created your empire? Developed a really good relationship? Or have you considered doing these things, only to think that watching the game with your buddies was a more important thing to do first?

Now, I am not telling you to not watch the game with your buddies. But don't watch it if you're doing so to put off doing something that will enrich your life in a bigger way! There is never a perfect time for anything, so why not live now?

It is common among so many people that we live as if we have forever on this planet. Have you ever met a person who had a near-death experience? Chances are, if you have—and have spoken with them—you will have observed that these people have a whole new outlook on life. They have a sense of urgency, a recognition of the little time we have, and a desire to make the most of it. We shouldn't need to have a near-death experience to be able to shift our thinking and value the time we have. You do, however, need to be willing to shift how you do things, how you structure your time, and how you can use your time to reach alignment in all areas of your life and, ultimately, to create total life satisfaction.

If your relationships are off, dedicate time to putting effort into reconnecting with all the people you love. Start with something simple like reaching out by writing a letter to someone, or inviting that friend you haven't seen in a long time for a cup a coffee. If your financial stability is off, devote time to focus on getting it on track. Consider setting up an appointment with a financial advisor to help you get a clear sense of the state of your finances. If your fitness level is poor, add a one-hour workout to each day and see how that changes your life. Instead of eating out, take the time to prepare a nutritious meal and see how that makes you feel. If your emotions feel misaligned, take time to care for yourself and cultivate emotional regulation daily through meditation, yoga, or journaling. It just takes one little step of change to send yourself in the direction you want to foster.

We all have the same twenty-four hours in a day. How you choose to spend your time makes all the difference in becoming the best-selling millionaire or continuing to remain stuck in your life by staying in front of the television. We all have the same amount of minutes in a day as Thomas Edison did, as Einstein, Mother Teresa, Gandhi, Steve Jobs, or Oprah! The difference between these people and you is not that they are better or different or magical; the difference is that they understood that time is precious, and they used time wisely and effectively to implement their vision and purpose in life. Ultimately, how these people chose to use their time served the world. The truth is, you can do it too, if you so choose. You have access to the same ingredients that these successful and well-known folks did.

Take a moment and visualize a long line with a "B" at one end and a "D" at the other end. The "B" is for birth, and the "D" is for death. If you are fifty years old, you might mark the middle of this line as your fifty-year time-point. Think back to the previous five years, from age forty-five to fifty. What goals did you achieve? What did you postpone or procrastinate on doing? Did you notice how fast those five years went by? If you think of your life in five-year increments, there are not many more before your potential expiration. The time to do what you want to do is now, and now is all there is.

The problem of procrastination and postponement, of waiting for something to happen before taking action, or waiting for "someday," is significant among so many people in the US today. This is perceived as apathy or laziness in the extreme. However, it is more revealing of fear; fear of failure, fear of success, fear of the unknown, fear of death, fear of change—the list goes on. Fear is often the underlying agent of much of our decision-making. It is also revealing of a culture of people who are not living in a state of awareness. Life is not meant for us to do by rote, living always on autopilot and waiting for things to happen to us.

We are the creators of our lives, for better and for worse, and the more you are able to recognize this, the more you can create the life of your dreams. The more you understand that life happens right now, not tomorrow, not someday, but right now, the more you will be inspired to take action. Taking action is integral in achieving results. If you are always procrastinating and postponing things, even if you feel motivated and are applying all the techniques we will discuss in this book, you are not actually taking action. Action is the essential piece in the puzzle of creating your life, manifesting your desires, and accomplishing great feats. By action, I mean implementing change in your daily life habits. You can change your subconscious programming all you want, but without also taking action and stepping fully into your life, you simply will not see results. It is pivotal that you apply the results of your 'changed' subconscious in your everyday lived experiences.

Procrastination only serves fear, and keeps you stuck in the life you are outgrowing as you become more aware. Imagine if Henry Ford had procrastinated or postponed his idea for making an automobile—cars nowadays might only look like they did in the sixties. We certainly would not have the electric car, and we may not have cars at all! Imagine if Bill Gates had procrastinated on creating Microsoft, or Steve Jobs postponed creating Apple, computer technology would be nowhere near what it is today. Each one of us is a unique and gifted soul with treasures to share with our families, our friends, our colleagues, indeed, with the world. When you procrastinate, you prevent yourself from sharing with anyone. How can you expect the accolades to come tumbling in when you postpone sharing what you are with the world?

Developing awareness about how you live each day is the best way to overcome these tendencies to procrastinate and postpone. We need to be constantly in a state of awareness, always on the lookout for what impedes progress in our lives. Is your life in perfect alignment? If any aspect of your life is out of kilter, be it your relationships, health, or financial well-being, then every aspect is affected, whether you are aware of this or not. If you are not aware of what is out of kilter, then you cannot bring everything back into alignment. However, if you know right away that your health is off and that this is affecting your relationships and financial situation, then you can take the necessary steps to bring everything back into order.

Consider the entrepreneur—entrepreneurs are another good example of people living in a state of awareness daily. Every entrepreneur knows that it is in their best interest to stay aware, so that if opportunities present themselves they can then adjust their lives to take advantage of these opportunities. In the event they may need to make quick decisions, by remaining aware an entrepreneur can seize any opportunity at a moment's notice. We can learn a lot from this type of approach to life. There is a necessary sense of urgency that we would do well to apply to life that helps us realize the value inherent in each day, hour, and minute.

We are all dying, from the moment we are born. There will never be a perfect time for anything. Life is full of broken fingers, broken hearts, broken cars, and some of the biggest regrets people have faced throughout the century have been around not doing something while they still had the chance. It is all too easy, especially in our culture of "work until you're 65, then retire and see the world," to remain rooted in procrastination and postponement, waiting for that magic "someday" to appear. This will only serve to limit you from experiencing life in a deep and rich way. Why wait until you're 65 to start living? Why wait until tomorrow, for that matter? Life is here right now, in this moment, as you read this book. What is it you most want to do? Ask yourself honestly, what are your deepest desires? You may feel limited by money, sure, this is common, and it might be your reality at the moment. But you are truly not limited by time, regardless of the story you tell yourself regarding time and what time is available to you.

The majority of people tend to get caught up in the day-to-day trivialities, such as paying their bills. Now, paying your bills might seem monumentally important to you, but honestly, can you think of anyone who has ever reported that they were successful in life because they mastered the art of bill paying? I am not saying that you shouldn't pay your bills. What I am saying is that it is important to catch yourself when you get caught up in something trivial and make it something big, so that you can use it as an excuse for not doing the really important things in life. Through healthy self-awareness, you can gain a clearer perspective and build healthy balance and organize your priorities in ways that serve you the most. At the end of your life, no one is going to remember whether or not you paid all of your bills and what a wonderful job you did of it. In other words, people get caught up in making a living instead of creating a life. They come to the end of their lives dissatisfied because they realize they only lived 10% of their lives, not because they were not capable or intelligent, and not for a lack of knowledge, but simply because they never had a clear idea about what they wanted.

So many people reside in this "woulda, coulda, shoulda" approach to life! Don't let this be you. Life is what is happening to you right now, and you are not a victim of life, but a creator. Life is yours to create. Are you an artist interested in creating a life masterpiece? Or are you a part of the crowd, creating a paint-by-numbers piece where the numbers are pre-designed by something, anything, that is not you? It is the simplest way to express it—we are all dying, but tragically, many of us are not actually living.

Fear, ignorance, and other long-running programs in the subconscious are what keep us in this state of procrastination or postponement. Once we begin to clear our deepest fears—known or unknown—and our ignorance about what we are capable of can we then start to live fully in each moment. The limiting beliefs or life lessons you learned and absorbed into your subconscious from when you were born might seem as though they want you to hang on to these ways of living, but it does not serve you to put off for tomorrow what you can do today.

When you are fully engaged in your life and really going for it full-out, you will feel the sense of urgency that life demands. When you live with awareness of how much time you have and the endless opportunity that exists in each minute, you have a much greater chance of aligning all aspects of your life and living in a state of fulfillment. There is no final destination; you decide whether to enjoy the journey or struggle constantly with it. Quite simply, the 'journey' of our lives is all that we are given. It is the most profound gift the universe grants us. If you keep waiting for the right time or the right circumstances to present themselves, you will surely wait forever. The right time is when you decide to act; the right circumstances are when you finally engage in the moment. Happiness is not something that comes along once we have all our ducks in a row; happiness is navigating the roller coaster of our lives and coming out ahead. Enjoy the ride, not the endpoint. This is why we need to be urgent and aware in our lives. Time is precious and life truly is short.

Growing awareness of the urgency of life, becoming aware of the need to repaint the canvas, and looking ahead to where you are going are all preliminary elements of the work that will change your life. Choosing to engage in subconscious mind programming techniques like the ones I will share in subsequent chapters in this book will further round out your ability to live your best life, not tomorrow, not next year, but the minute you put this book down.

Chapter Eight: Why you are the "Other People"

By now, you may be starting to see just how the patterns, thoughts, and corresponding emotions picked up by the subconscious throughout your life have affected you. There are all kinds of things you do in a day that are directly dictated by thoughts and programming that you were never aware of until you read this book. Living life without awareness or treating it like the precious gift it is may be one way this programming shows up for you in your daily life. Another phenomenon I see more often than not when people show up to my seminars is what I call the myth of the "Other People." This is when you separate yourself from the people in society who have what you want; the so-called "Other People." I've got news for all of you that have experienced this kind of thinking: You *are* the "Other People."

Have you ever seen a Maserati and thought, "That's not for me, it's for other people"? This is what I am talking about. I come across people all the time who truly believe that fame, success, nice homes, Mercedes-Benz cars—you name it—they're all for the "Other People." To all of you who think this way, I ask: Who are these "Other People?" Where did they come from? Do they live on another planet? More importantly, why are you not the "Other People?"

I mean it when I say *you are* the "Other People." I imagine some of you reading this are shaking your head, and remaining convinced that no, that nice house is not for you, but let me assure you—it is. So is the Maserati, so is the Prada dress, so is the country home. It doesn't even have to be material things! Have you ever found yourself thinking that financial security or peaceful relationships are for the "Other People"? Or being fit and healthy, is that for the "Other People" too?

Thinking this way is limiting on so many levels. Thinking this way keeps you identifying with a group, rather than as an individual. And the group you identify with, according to you, is who? Not the "Other People," presumably. You segregate yourself culturally when you give in to this kind of limited thinking. You also omit and entirely disregard your own ability to acquire the things you want. Without realizing it, you are disempowering yourself. Every time you engage in this kind of thinking, you are reinforcing a subconscious barrier that reminds you of all that you cannot have. Your mind engages in limiting self-talk, which has a big impact on how you can achieve your goals. If you are always telling yourself that the "Other People" have wealth, and you cannot have it because you are not the "Other People," then you are keeping yourself in a limitation—all based on a belief or perception that may not have been yours in the first place! Remember, you were born into this world and your mind was a blank canvas. Where did you really learn there were "Other People" and where did you really learn that you were not one of them?

The danger in this kind of thinking is that we begin to live vicariously through the "Other People." Take for example our culture's addiction to celebrity. How many of us read magazines and watch 'reality' TV shows about people who seem to have all of the things we think we will never be able to have. I have heard people say on several occasions "I get to work on a great mansion." To which I say, why don't you own the great mansion? Why is this for someone else? We look at who we believe to be the "Other People" in the world and bestow upon them our energy instead of replenishing our own wellspring. We wear sports jerseys with other people's names on them, even buying them at $100 apiece. What about making that sports jersey with your own name on it? What is stopping you from doing that? Imagine what your life could be like if you prioritized yourself, if you invested the energy you give away to those 'other people' into yourself.

If you give yourself a break from self-defeating thoughts and limiting beliefs, and truly look around at the world, you will find that not everyone whom you might classify as "Other People" is smarter than you. Not all of them are handsome, in great shape, or have outstanding relationships. What they do have, however, is that sense of urgency and zest for life. They do not procrastinate, and get on with fulfilling their dreams. They work hard, and they work smart, all things you are able to do as well. They are indeed humans, on this planet, not unlike you in so many fundamental ways. The world was born out of people's thoughts and creativity, and if people had not shared their thoughts and creativity, we would not have a fraction of the infrastructure and technology we enjoy today in the world. You are a unique representation of spirit, the divine, creator, universe, source, Universal Power—any way you refer to it, it is you. All that you dream and desire is yours for the taking if you step out of this segregated way of thinking and step into the fact that you are the "Other People."

Why is it that you can have a person who seems to have superior abilities, talents, skills, and education, while at the same time, they don't produce the quality of life they want or that you might expect from them? Why is it, on the other hand, you can have someone who seemingly has every disadvantage—no family support, the wrong social status, no emotional support, no education, and the wrong background—yet they go out and produce results way beyond what anyone could have expected or even imagined?

What is it that keeps you in this mode of thinking? Simply put, it is doubt. Doubt is like a cognitive cancer of the mind. For example, if you have a gallon of spring water and you put just one drop of cyanide in that gallon, the entire gallon is poisoned. This is how doubt affects us—if you have a spirit full of enthusiasm and motivation, but somehow one drop of doubt gets into your spirit, your entire spirit is poisoned with doubt. The only way to overcome doubt is to use the strategies I outline in this book to deal directly with the subconscious mind, and then create barriers that do not allow any seeds of doubt to take root.

When we persist in believing there are "Other People," and they are not us, we can then rationalize our own existence and give ourselves an excuse to wallow in self-pity. I'm here to tell you, the wallowing gets you nowhere. If your identity is inextricably tied up in separating yourself from the "Other People," you must get ready to redefine yourself.

After all, what the heck does identity mean anyway? It can be such a big and often loaded word. Well, as I said in chapter one, I believe identity is the strongest force in the human personality. If you want to know what shapes you the most, it's not your capability. It's your identity and the rules you have for who you think you are. Most of us defined ourselves a long time ago. When we step outside that definition, we get really uncomfortable, because the strongest force in the human personality is the need to remain consistent with how we define ourselves. One of our human needs is certainty. So if certainty is one of the deepest needs we have, if you don't know who you are, you don't know how to act. This is one of the main reasons we resist change, because it involves stepping into the unknown, completely away from certainty.

Very early in life, we began to define who we are. We used labels such as loner, aggressive, conservative, sexy, successful, loser, rich, poor, in charge. I work for others. I am ugly. I am smart. I am a procrastinator. I am clumsy. I am athletic. I am thin. I am big-boned. No doubt you can think of many more of these 'programming' identity statements that we use. What happens is that these definitions become self-fulfilling prophecies, because nobody wants to be disappointed. Nobody wants to live in a place of uncertainty. This is how you find yourself, spending your whole life talking about how the car you most desire is not for you, but for the "Other People."

Another piece of this phenomenon of thought is the concept of our internal thermostats. This is a metaphor that is often used when we talk about our comfort zones. The idea is that your comfort zone is like a thermostat. We all have our comfort zone, and it is set by the subconscious mind. So if your subconscious mind has set your thermostat in a particular area of your life, for example, how much money you make, and let's say it is set at 45 degrees, if the temperature drops down to 40 degrees, guess what happens? It doesn't meet your identity. If the only kind of love you knew as a child was abuse, or the only kind of life you knew was living paycheck to paycheck and being in debt, or the only kind of lifestyle you ever experienced was sedentary, whatever it is, even though it might be painful, it is what you know. This becomes your comfort zone and therefore provides the certainty that you need. It becomes your self-definition and what you think you deserve. You begin to think, not consciously but unconsciously, that this *is* love, this is just the body you inherited, or that wealth is for the "Other People," or you're not the right kind of person to make certain kinds of social contacts. Of course, this is not your conscious thinking. This is what is going on in your subconscious. This is why we often don't get the results we are after, or continue to sabotage the matter, regardless of what types of technology, techniques, and information we add to our bag of tricks.

The subconscious mind, and subsequently the identity you have formed, has a story about what you can and cannot achieve in the world, and this is demonstrated by your set-point on your internal thermostat. For example, have you ever noticed how some lottery winners have the money for about a year before it's all been blown? This is because all these people may have known is a salary of $40,000. This is what they know they can manage, this is what they are comfortable with, and this is what their thermostat is set at. For people like this, winning a million dollars enters them into a whole new playing field, one that is well out of their comfort zones. Winning that amount of money propels the winners directly into the unknown. Usually what happens next is the money is blown, squandered, or improperly managed until—surprise—they end up back at $40,000. Essentially, they unconsciously made decisions and choices that returned them to their 'original' set-point/comfort zone.

Another example is in relationships. So many people repeat relationship patterns again and again without even being aware that is what they're doing. Some people's relationship thermostat is set to cruise control, where they enter into a relationship that is void of passion or any kind of emotional roller coaster. When the relationship does become passionate or dramatic, they're out. They retreat back into the relationship that fits their thermostat—comfortable, with no ripples, and no passion. The opposite is true here too—some people chase the drama, or the feeling of "new love," or a real roller-coaster ride, and once the relationship settles into being drama-free, trusting, or comfortable, they are out of it and retreat back to seeking relationships full of adventure.

Even when we look at health, we have our thermostats set. Especially when you consider weight, generally a loaded subject and very much an ingrained part of some people's identities. Some people carry a story around that they are "big-boned" and cannot weigh less than a certain amount. Guess what happens to these people? No matter how hard they try, their weight bounces back, whether up or down, to the set-point that their weight-belief thermostat set for them, regardless of their awareness of it. This is partly why fad diets simply do not work; once the diet has achieved its goal and the person has lost weight, it's just a matter of time before they regain the weight. Without changing their fundamental beliefs about weight or aspects of their identities that are tied to weight, and re-setting the thermostat, no long-term weight loss can be achieved.

Whatever it is, when you drop below your comfort zone, you will be compelled to re-correct it, automatically. If your body gets out of control and you lose too much weight, there is a point at which you might think, "That's enough!" You are willing to be a little off your identity, but not that much. That's when suddenly you change and gain weight back, because you feel the pressure that comes with being inconsistent with your own definition of how you think you should be.

Whether you are re-correcting to stay the same weight, or re-correcting to stay in the same income bracket, or in the same type of relationship, realize that this is not your *goal*. Your goal is something much larger. This pattern of re-correcting is directly connected to your subconscious comfort zone or your subconscious definition of yourself. Even if it gets better than you expected, perhaps you lose a lot of weight and get into really good shape, or perhaps you lead your company in sales for two quarters in a row when you normally come in third or fourth, or perhaps you jump from 70 degrees in your intimacy, and now you have a relationship that is at 90 or even 100 degrees. You have a really hot, passionate relationship with more passion than you have ever had before, or you lose three dress sizes instead of one, or you double your income, whatever it is, your subconscious mind starts talking to you. Then your brain goes, "Hello, dude what the heck are you doing? You are a 70-degree guy, what are you doing way up here at 90 degrees? You can't keep that. That's not going to last. Get back down to 70 degrees before you get hurt or fail or screw it up. You're in over your head. You're not an entrepreneur. You work for other people." On and on it goes, as your identity—crafted by your subconscious, crafted by other people's thoughts, beliefs, and programming—strives to maintain itself as you best know it to be. Wherever your subconscious mind has set your comfort zone based on the way you define yourself, you're going to keep adjusting to stay in that comfort zone. So many times in so many personal development programs, people challenge you to get out of your comfort zone, which you can't do consciously. You have to go into your subconscious and reset your comfort zone, just like you would the thermostat. And this will keep happening until you reprogram your subconscious mind with a new identity, and a new comfort zone. Before you set out to make any kind of lasting change, you must reset your subconscious comfort zone.

Without resetting your comfort zone, if you continue to move out of it and achieve success, then the drive to make things better stops. You stop growing and gradually you drift back until you are once again in your comfort zone. Worse, you may start to sabotage yourself—the mental air conditioners kick in and bring you right back down to where you think you deserve to be, based on your subconscious identity and the expectations that result.

This is where the shortcomings with many of the programs you may have tried in the past are evident. There are a plethora of programs out there designed to pump you up and feel good about it. Programs like these motivate you with affirmations and teach you to use visualization. They may have even taught you that the universal laws work for everyone. You may have made some changes, but it is highly likely that these changes did not last. When you are taught these things, you know and are assimilating all you've learned in your head, on a conscious level. However, your identity and self-definition is set by the subconscious mind, so before you can make any substantive or lasting change, first you must reprogram your subconscious mind and change who you are at the deepest level.

I invite you to step into being the "Other People" by charting a new course for your identity. If you keep reading this book, you will see in subsequent chapters how to move deeper into your own self-awareness, so that by the time you reach chapter twelve, you will be ready to integrate the Rules of the Mind into your life, and by the time you get to chapter fourteen, you will be more than ready to amplify the power of this technology. Despite what you may have been led to believe, your identity can be changed, and along with it all limiting and non-useful patterns, programming, and beliefs that keep you thinking the world is full of you, and 'them.' Become the "Other People" and own the success and achievements you're capable of!

If you want to create a life that you feel is full, enriching, and satisfying to you, it is important to notice these two tendencies in yourself. If you constantly tell yourself you are undeserving of what the "Other People" have, you will remain without whatever it is you think you want. If you don't take steps to deactivate and reprogram your internal thermostat—on all levels—you will find that no matter what you do, you will return to your comfort setting every time.

Maybe it's time to take another look at who you are today. And maybe you don't have to actually give up your identity. Maybe the identity of created for yourself is magnificent, but maybe it's time to expand it. Maybe it's time to add to it. Maybe it's time to open up to a new level of freedom and options. And when you do that, there will be a processional effect in all areas of your life, because we are all connected in a cybernetic loop. If I want to change you, I can try to control you, but that will not change anything. Or I can try to change the system, but that will either be futile, or it will not last. Or, I can change me into an identity where everything changes. For example, if I change the way I treat you, the way I respond to you, my voice, my body, my feelings, and my emotions, my respect for you, it will affect the way you feel and the way you respond to me. The same is true with the universe and higher intelligence. Once you change yourself, reprogram your subconscious mind, and become the person you need to become to achieve the things that you want in your life, then you will begin to receive a different response from the universe in a different result in your life. Then you begin to experience your life as a masterpiece.

What we value controls what we are willing to do or not do—in our businesses, and our relationships, with our bodies and with her children. Some people get locked in place into a particular mindset. I call it being committed to your commitment. For example, have you ever been in an argument and you were so angry that as the argument progressed, you forgot what you were angry about, and it just became about winning? We've all been there and what happens is we get committed to being angry instead of resolving the argument. Or we get committed to being right, instead of uncovering the truth. When this happens, we get so wrapped up in our commitment that we can no longer see the forest through the trees. We lose touch with what we really want, because we get stuck in a mindset and we get committed to our commitments. This is just a reflection of how committed we are to our identities and how locked in place we are when we get so entrenched in them.

Instead of staying locked into whatever identity you feel most comfortable in, I want you to start to think, feel, and believe fully that you are, in fact, the "Other People." Who are you to be otherwise? If we were all born as pure spirit, and we all have the same amount of minutes in each day, what is the difference between you being a creator of your life, and someone you think of as the "Other Person"? The difference lies in the thoughts you think. When you believe you cannot have things but "Other People" can, you are the one limiting yourself, no one else. You engage in that kind of thinking, and feel the resultant emotions, and manifest the expected result, which is not having the things the "Other People" have. What if one day you changed that thought pattern? What would your life look like if you really stepped into being the "Other People"? How different would things be for you? Fear and doubt exist in all of us, from the poorest person to a millionaire. It is part of the human condition. How you choose to respond to fear and doubt is what will allow you to step out of limiting thinking—like believing in this whole "Us and Them" approach—and step into full responsibility for being the creator of your life.

Choose to step into being the "Other People," because that is how I already see you. Nobody is perfect, no one has this game of life "right" and all tied up in a pretty box with a bow. Own your whole self—your light, your dark, your conscious, your subconscious. Own all of the patterns you have running in the background of your subconscious mind—and then work to eliminate the emotional connection from these. You are the master of your own life, and only you can make the changes you need to allow the limitless abundance—abundance that the universe wants you to have—come to you effortlessly.

Part 3: Becoming Your Mind's Architect

Chapter Nine: Hypnosis as a Way to Access Our Hidden Potential

At this point, you may be wondering what exactly hypnosis is, and why it is effective. What is the connection between hypnosis and the subconscious mind?

Hypnosis works by altering our state of consciousness. It acts as a bridge between the conscious mind (beta) and subconscious (theta) mind. The origins of hypnosis can be traced as far back as ancient civilizations like the Egyptian, early Greek, Roman, Chinese, Persian, and Sumerian peoples. Ancient documents show that hypnosis was used as a therapeutic device to cure physical and emotional ailments and diseases. In the eighteenth century, Western explorers in the Far and Middle East encountered the practice of hypnosis and brought it back to the West. The most well-known of these exploratory scientists was Doctor Fantz Anton Mesmer of Austria. We still use the term 'mesmerize' today, a result of the impact of the work of this early pioneer of hypnosis. Armand de Puysegur, one of Mesmer's followers continuing his work, discovered that a state of trance could be induced via both direct commands and the spoken word.

Hypnosis involves producing, sometimes via inducing, a natural relaxed state of mind that encourages a connection between the conscious and subconscious parts of the mind, all while the person undergoing hypnosis remains fully conscious. What this also means is that someone in a state of hypnosis will not do something they wouldn't normally do. In this altered state, you are still entirely in control—it's just your focus and awareness that shifts. When the mind is in this altered or hypnotic state, it is more receptive to suggestions and new ideas, for in this state, the conscious mind is rendered less dominant and the subconscious mind becomes more accessible. In this relaxed state of mind, there is more opportunity to create an environment for sustainable change and the manifestation of your desires and outcomes because you are tapping right into the 'heart' of the matter; the subconscious mind.

Before delving deeper into the topic, let's revisit the states of the brain. Remember those four states we talked about earlier? Alpha, beta, theta, and delta. For the purposes of hypnosis, the focus is on the alpha and delta states of the brain. Alpha is the brain state we enter prior to falling asleep and pass through again upon waking up. Another time we may find ourselves in the alpha state is while engaging in daydreaming. Have you ever felt yourself completely absorbed in a waking dream state, and noticed yourself pleasantly drifting into an altered state? The alpha state is associated with a sense of pleasantness, contentment, and relaxation. Getting yourself into the alpha state is as simple as taking a few deep breaths, and becoming aware of your breathing and your body. To amplify the alpha state, a technique called 'fractional relaxation' is used. Fractional means just that, to divide the body into parts and focus your attention on relaxing each of those parts of the body one at a time. Often this is led by the sound of someone's voice outside of you. For instance, someone might say, "Begin by relaxing your head, next feel the tension release from your shoulders." You are still fully in control of this process; in fact, you are the 'agent' who is shifting your mind from one state to another. A willingness must be present in order for you to allow your mind to shift from one state to another. You may have heard your yoga teacher using the fractional relaxation technique to guide you into a deeper experience of savasana, or final relaxation pose, generally the last pose of every yoga class.

Focusing the mind on specifically relaxing different parts of the body achieves three different things. First, the person becomes more relaxed. Relaxation is an important component of how effective hypnosis can be. Second, fractional relaxation shifts your awareness to the process of relaxation at the exclusion of everything else. Your mind becomes focused on this task and sets aside the other ideas and thoughts it may have been circulating. A good example to illustrate what the mind is experiencing here is that of a magnifying glass. The mind is concentrated and absorbed closely on one task, while the outside elements remain present. A magnifying glass works in the same way, concentrating the rays of the sun to a pointed, more powerful focus. Hypnosis works in a similar fashion, enabling us to use our minds like a powerful tool with which we can then plant information in the subconscious mind, where it can be carried into our lives through action. Essentially, your mind becomes more clear and much more focused. Another occurrence during this process is that of the conscious mind taking a 'backseat' to the subconscious mind. You are, of course, still totally aware of what is happening around you, but your awareness is softened and less rigid; your awareness becomes primarily focused on what is happening inside your mind as opposed to outside your body.

Use of the theta brain waves are also an integral part of hypnosis. Theta brain waves are the waves that the brain generates in deep states of meditation. Theta is also the place where lucid dreaming occurs. As you become more relaxed, some theta waves may be produced. Bear in mind that the states of the mind are not exclusive. You may be in the alpha state, but have some theta waves being produced. In reality, each of us moves in and out of various mind states throughout our days. As the process of hypnosis deepens and you experience a deepened sense of relaxation and a heightened sense of internal focus, more theta waves will be produced by the brain to reflect this. Once you have entered this 'hypnotic' state, you are now ready to work with the subconscious mind. Remember that the subconscious mind really responds to visual and emotional information.

Hypnosis puts you into a relaxed, meditative, and trance-like state. In this state, you are more in alignment with your source-self, you are more connected to that Universal Power and, most especially, you are in vibrational alignment. When the mind is in a hypnotic state, it is capable of becoming hyper-focused, as well as being highly suggestible and receptive. Have you ever seen someone deeply absorbed in a daydream, or, indeed, have you seen someone being hypnotized? They often appear 'tuned out' or in a state of trance. This is because so much of the person's focus is internal. The person may appear not to be paying attention, but the truth is they are paying very close attention to their own internal landscape. Essentially, when we are hypnotized, we are hyper-focused on self-generated imagery, or imagery that is suggested by someone outside of us. While we are in this deeply absorbed state, we effectively circumnavigate the conscious mind to interact directly with the subconscious mind. Our conscious mind is often the place of our sense of self-judgment, or self-generated resistance. These are some of the results of earlier experiences that can produce self-limiting habit patterns that embed themselves in the subconscious. Thankfully, the subconscious is reprogrammable! This is another reason hypnosis is so powerful. By communicating directly with the subconscious mind, you can plant new ideas, concepts, and habits that the conscious mind may derail in your usual awake, or beta, state. The subconscious is also the habit mechanism of our minds. When you are working with the intention to build new habits into your life and to bring your goals and dreams closer to you, you need to work effectively with the subconscious mind.

The efficacy of hypnosis is also related to the clarity and strength of your desire. Your desire (and your desired outcome) must be accompanied by a very clear intention of what it is that you want to create or achieve. Your subconscious mind favors clarity. If you do not know what it is that you want, you can't count on getting the cooperation of the subconscious mind. Without clear messaging to your subconscious, how can your subconscious mind enable you to make changes in your life? Consider your desired outcome like plants in a garden and your subconscious mind like the soil of the garden. Your seeds are like the ideas that you plant in the garden. Every seed is engineered to produce a plant, given the right kind of soil and correct nurturing. Just as the gardener plants the seed into the soil, with a faithful knowing that it will become a plant, so too do you need to have faith that your outcomes, through clearly articulated intentions, will come to be. It is also very important that you keep a relaxed approach to the whole process. The subconscious mind really favors a relaxed state of being and the more we can cultivate and remain in this state of being, the more easily our desired outcomes get created.

Another essential ingredient to successfully drawing your desires to you is commitment. Stay focused on your goals, and commit to staying the course of their fruition. Commitment also means that you stay focused on the end result while staying with the whole course of steps and circumstances as they unfold themselves closer and closer to your desired outcome. Every garden needs tending to in order for the seeds to germinate and grow into healthy plants. Your ability to harvest the fruits of your intentions and desires is directly related to your dedication to the process from start to finish. Your job is to keep your eyes on the horizon of your destination, and fuel your journey with regular practice. What kind of practice? The practice of using imagery, emotion, and a relaxed state of mind to feed your dreams and desires.

Let's illustrate this with an example. Fred is a divorced businessman in his late fifties. He works sixty hours a week, hardly ever exercises, and grabs his take-out lunch from the diner around the corner from his office about five times a week. Fred sincerely wants to get healthier by exercising and eating more nutritious food and he wants to be actively dating women again. Fred knows that his weight is a major factor in his self-confidence and also a big factor in why he has not been dating.

What to do for Fred? First, we need to create an imagery and feelings for Fred that he associates with his goals; his primary goals being to become healthier and gain the confidence to start dating again. Then, we need to have Fred get into a relaxed state. Fred can even do this at the office, sitting at his desk chair. As Fred's body relaxes, we need him to focus his attention on his breath, while letting go of all other thoughts in his head. He needs to be encouraged to continue focusing on his breath and to draw his attention inside of himself, letting go of his external environment.

From this state, we can help Fred out by having him bring to mind an image of himself when he was more trim. We need Fred to bring to mind how he feels about this more slender 'version' of himself. Now Fred has an image of himself as healthy and less overweight and this image is accompanied by positive feelings about himself. Words that Fred may say to himself during the hypnotic state could be, "I feel stronger and more self-confident when I choose healthier foods" or "I have the confidence to date attractive potential mates when I take care of my own health needs."

To amplify the power of this image, let's bring in an attractive date for Fred. Now, as Fred is continuing to relax, he is absorbed in the image of himself as fit and healthy, accompanied by feeling self-confident, and also in this image he is sitting across the table from an attractive woman in an elegant restaurant. To really entrench this idea even further into Fred's subconscious mind, we can have Fred imagine in clear detail what his date looks like, the smell of the food on the plates on the restaurant table, and the image of the two glasses of red wine at the place settings. We would continue to encourage Fred to notice the positive feelings that arise from imagining this scenario.

Because the subconscious mind is such a habit-loving mechanism, it's important that Fred revisit this scenario with a relaxed state of mind frequently, at least once a day. It's also important that Fred connect to a sense of faith in the process itself, and faith that the seeds of his ideas will plant themselves into his subconscious. In this example, we have all of the ingredients of a successful hypnosis session. There is a clear desire, in that Fred wants to slim down and eat healthier so that he feels confident to date attractive women. Fred's intention is also clear: He wants to become healthier so that he can date good-looking potential mates. Faith and commitment are also present in this example. Fred is committed to his outcome, and to the process involved, and he has a faith in its success.

Of course, Fred is not going to go from a 47-inch waist to a 40-inch waist overnight! By continuously revisiting the imagery of his confident self at the restaurant table sitting across from the attractive woman and noticing the feelings that he has as he brings this image to mind, Fred is reinforcing the ability to cultivate new and healthier habits. How is this effective? Because Fred is using two components that the subconscious mind loves—imagery and emotion. These give his goals a substance that the subconscious mind can digest. Let's have Fred do his practice in the mornings, while he's in the alpha state, just as he's waking. At lunchtime, when Fred is deciding where to go for lunch and what to have, the effects of his self-hypnosis will have planted some new seeds in his subconscious. As Fred considers where to eat lunch, he briefly brings to mind the image of himself in the restaurant. He remembers the strength of his desire in wanting this outcome to manifest in his life. And, he feels the good feeling of sitting at a table with a desirable date! This time, Fred chooses a salad bar around the corner from the diner and gets in a little bit of exercise at the same time. Fred's usual decision-making process before doing this work wasn't so much of a true moment of decision as it was just acting out of habit by default. By planting the seeds of his desired outcome in his subconscious mind on a regular basis, he is supporting himself to cultivate and sustain new and different habits. He is enabling himself to consciously build habits into his life that will support him in reaching his goals.

The power we have within us is truly formidable, and thanks to these pioneers in the field of hypnosis, thousands upon thousands of people throughout the ages have undergone tremendous healings on the mental, emotional, and physical level just by changing the thoughts and beliefs held in the subconscious mind. Inducing the mind into a state of relaxation, and pairing it with clarity of desire, and commitment to achieving the desire, is a clear route to re-patterning the mind and achieving goals. Now, with the techniques and strategies that I am about to share with you, in the spirit of my forbearers, you don't even have to go out of your home and pay a hypnotist to make changes today. I am talking about changes that will benefit your life by helping to bring you into full alignment across every aspect of your life—finances, relationships, emotional health, physical health, and well-being.

Chapter Ten: The Power of Suggestion

Part of what makes hypnosis so effective as a tool to reprogram the subconscious mind is the fact that it calls upon the power of suggestion. In hypnosis, the hypnotist induces the almost trancelike state of relaxation in his or her client in order to create the conducive environment (the garden) in which to plant positive suggestions (the seeds). For many people, hypnosis is effective to help quit smoking, for example. The hypnotist simply plants the suggestion to cease smoking in the garden of the client's mind, after the garden has been tilled and made ready for planting, of course. This is but one example of the power of suggestion being effective for people who seek the help of hypnotists.

It is important to recognize that the power of suggestion is truly everywhere. One need only look at the world of advertising to see just how strong and insidious the power of suggestion really is. This is why it is vital that you recognize this as truly the power it is. Children watching television are being given suggestions constantly about which toys they might want or foods they might want to eat. The same goes for adults, to be sure, and there are many, many subtleties in the language of suggestion that are known to all who are clever in the marketing and advertising fields. Indeed, there is a significant art to the act of persuasion, and people in sales, in particular, often learn several tricks of the trade geared towards capturing your attention, and making the sale they want. In your personal life, you can either harness the power of suggestion and use it to suggest positive and affirming thoughts to your mind or you can continue to be prey to all of those using the power of suggestion to convince you to buy or do things, everywhere you go, on a daily basis!

We have incredible imaginations, and a subconscious mind that responds to visualization. We have the ability to bring to mind visually whatever it is people tell us to think. If I say, "Think of an elephant," chances are quite good right now you are thinking of an elephant. If I say, "Think of an elephant with a little man in a purple velvet coat riding it," you are likely picturing that. We can't help it—it's how the human mind works. Even if I say, "Don't think of an elephant," guess what? You likely still thought of an elephant. We have active and dynamic imaginations that can create pictures at the invitation of what people are telling us. We take in suggestions like this, and while we cannot always control what people are suggesting to us, with awareness of what is happening, namely, that we are being given a suggestion, we can observe our minds and choose to hold the visual or not in that moment. Further, we can work with this fascinating aspect of the human mind to suggest to ourselves how we want our lives to go.

Now, take this information and recall what I said earlier regarding how the subconscious mind accepts at face value whatever it is you are thinking in the conscious mind. Repetition of the thought in the conscious mind also reinforces the thought in the subconscious mind. Recall how the subconscious mind also cannot extract the negative. Consider, now, how tremendous the power of suggestion really is. Everything you are saying, everything you are hearing and, crucially, everything you are thinking is being taken in by your subconscious mind as suggestion. The subconscious mind is also the access point to the omnipotent power within, which is expansive and creative, and therefore just wants to create that which is suggested. Are you beginning to see why it is so absolutely essential to get a handle on not only what you are thinking, but how you are now filtering everything that you take in from the world around you?

It is small wonder that in today's society our minds think the way they do. When you think about any messages that you have heard repeatedly throughout the course of your life, whether from your parents or the media, it's really any wonder you can change your subconscious mind at all! Suggestion runs deep, from your parents telling you the ways of the world, to the media telling you all kinds of messages about gender, race, politics, religious beliefs, what's hot, what's not, and on and on and on. Have you ever stopped to wonder why exactly it is that you want that new pair of Nike shoes? Did you even think you might want them before you saw the billboard driving to work, or the ad on television? Yet there you are, buying new Nike shoes. Or the latest iPad. Or even a Big Mac for dinner. Chances are high that all of these decisions came from you being susceptible to the suggestions of the ads of these companies.

Using this as an example of just how susceptible we are to the power of suggestion, now consider how you might realign your life using the power of suggestion. Before I proceed with actual practical techniques you can apply in working with the subconscious mind, I want to impress upon you the importance of fully understanding not only the power of suggestion, but the use of auto-suggestion.

Auto-suggestion is the primary tool in reintegrating positive and supportive thoughts. As opposed to searching out a hypnotist to plant the suggestions into your mind, with auto-suggestion, you can do it yourself. In the next chapter, I will explain a practical technique for auto-suggestion in more detail.

You can begin to work with auto-suggestion at any time. You do not even need to believe it will work, or believe the suggestions you are making at first! As the subconscious mind integrates with each repetition, soon the belief will also become integrated. Don't let the fact that you do not believe—yet—that which you are trying to tell yourself stop you from beginning the practice. Life is for living right now. You are reading this book for a reason—perhaps you had a flash of intuition when you picked this book up, or you felt somehow called to open its pages. Regardless, whether you believe in auto-suggestion or not, whether you believe you will be rich one day or not, whether you believe the love you seek is available to you or not, I ask you this: What harm does it do to begin programming your mind to believe these things today? In this moment?

Once you realize how the subconscious mind is so incredibly easily influenced by suggestion, you may start to shift some of your habits in life. You may listen to a different radio station, one with less commercials, perhaps. You may choose to stop watching television altogether. You will notice your own language and how it affects what is drawn to you. For example, if you say to yourself and others that you do not have this or that, even if it is followed by an expression of strong desire to have this or that, you are still announcing it in the negative to your subconscious mind. You will see, over time, just how imperative it is to hold the positive thoughts first and foremost in your mind, to use positive language, and to try to keep a positive external environment around you (insofar as that is possible).

Take a look around in your life and see how the power of suggestion is at work around you. You can use it yourself, and for good, not evil! The power of suggestion, coupled with hypnosis, is at the heart of reprogramming the subconscious mind. Using auto-suggestion effectively can profoundly alter your life. Even if you don't believe in the suggestions you are giving yourself yet, with persistent, clear, and committed practice using auto-suggestion, you can truly manifest all that which you desire. In the next two chapters, I will go over a few world-class subconscious mind programming techniques that make use of auto-suggestion to get you started.

Chapter Eleven: Adjusting the Mind

You are the one you are with, 24/7, 365. Your internal influence is so fundamental to how you operate in each moment. The question now becomes, how do you actually adjust your mind so that you can achieve optimum functioning on a daily basis? In fact, not just optimum functioning—all-out full-on vitality and achievement, daily, across all facets of your life! For this we have to turn to subconscious mind programming techniques. It is in adjusting the mind that you will truly be able to adjust your world. The more effort you begin to spend on using the techniques I am about to share with you, the more you will see results. You will see your life change in amazing and unthinkable ways, and much more swiftly than through using any other personal development techniques. You will see your life change on an entirely new level, and not only will you be creating change, but you will be creating sustainable change for your life. Who doesn't want that? What I am offering is not a quick fix, but it is a long-term and highly effective fix. Go for the long game—it always pays off.

By now, you get that your mind has two major players, the conscious mind and the subconscious mind. Your subconscious mind is like your GPS system, constantly running in the background. You conscious mind is like the steering wheel in the car. For many of us, we think we can take our hands off the steering wheel and let the car drive. What happens when we do this? Our GPS takes over and all of a sudden, all of those old limiting patterns, beliefs, and emotions take control. You may be driving along in life, feeling okay, when something happens, you take your hands off the wheel, your subconscious is triggered, and you are terrified or anxious without any understanding as to why. This is what happens when you are not in control of your conscious mind, the steering wheel of your life.

I explained in chapter three about how essential it is to live your life with awareness, and this applies even more so when you want to start adjusting your mind. You must be aware. We do so many things in a day—brush our teeth, clean our bodies, prepare nourishing meals, you name it—to keep ourselves presentable and healthy. There are all kinds of little things we do daily in the name of hygiene or keeping ourselves in good shape. Yet I have seen so many people— too many, in my opinion—who completely neglect their mental and emotional health! We take such good care to look good and feel good physically, but spend no time cultivating sound mental and emotional health. So you have to be aware of your thoughts and how you think, and integrate some techniques into your life daily if you want to truly make some changes.

Living life unconsciously, that is, letting your subconscious run along as it will, operating 24/7, and using your conscious mind to survive, will only lead to a life unfulfilled. This is a life that is mapped by continually looping and tripping on old habits and patterns. If you truly understand that within you is the power to do whatever you want in your life, then you will start to make it a priority to work on reprogramming your subconscious mind so that you can, in effect, get out of your own way.

Through these world-class subconscious reprogramming techniques, I will help you to get your subconscious functioning like a GPS that is your best buddy—your most potent ally! With some adjustments and fine-tuning, you can be rid of all the limiting stuff and position yourself to get on with it—creating your life as you really wish it to be. Just like eating the right things will contribute to good health on the physical level, so does thinking the right things contribute to good health on the mental and emotional levels. Being aligned in all areas of your life allows you to thrive completely. You can launch yourself out of survival mode and into thriving when you adjust your subconscious mind.

I want to share two simple techniques with you for adjusting the mind, but before I do, I want to impress upon you the importance of controlling the environment around you. It is not only your internal environment that is influencing you in each moment; indeed, the external environment is highly influential as well.

Recall that there are three ways the mind has been programmed. There was programming by authority, by traumatic incident, and by repetition. Inherent in each of these is the importance of environment. If you really want to expedite reprogramming your subconscious mind, it is imperative that you pay attention to the environment around you.

For instance, say you really want to get in shape. You work pretty hard at it, going to the gym an hour a day. Chances are you will be more motivated to stay disciplined and work hard at it if you are surrounded by people who are in good shape and stay active. If you find that your friend group is mostly made up of people who are overweight and choose sedentary activities over being active, you might find it more difficult to get into shape. That environment is not conducive to you being in great shape and is counterproductive in moving you towards your goal of being in great shape.

If you are driving a car down a road and the road is doing nothing but kicking up dirt and sand on the windshield, you might consider driving down a different road. It is as simple as that. Anything in your external environment that is not contributing to the desired end-result, anything that is not in alignment with your goals, must be changed.

This becomes a challenge when we look at the people in our lives. The people in our lives make up our interactive environment. You can and must control your interactive environment. It is imperative that you be selective and discerning about the people that you spend time with. Again, consider the role of the bouncer. Other people have a huge influence on us, and how we think about ourselves. You may have friends and family that are loving and supportive. These people emotionalize the feelings of love and encouragement in you. Look at whom you spend time with on a regular basis. Are these people positive or are they critical? You may have friends or family that try to hold you back, are negative, or criticize you constantly. These people are detracting from your environment and impacting your ability to get what you want. This is when the tough decisions have to come in—one of which might mean moving away from these people, or decreasing the amount of time you spend with them. If you cannot physically get space from toxic people, you can just tune them out. Turn the volume down in your mind's ear so that you no longer hear the negative comments. Turn the volume up once something positive to your ears appears. Keep in mind that like attracts like and try as much as you can to control what you take in at the auditory and visual levels. Work with the idea of feeding and nourishing your goals and dreams by choosing and creating an environment that supports them. You want to build an external map that helps cue you and reminds you of what your desired results are as you are building the internal map that will attract more things to support that which you want to manifest.

Another part of the environment around you is the spatial environment. You can control the space you are in to some degree, although not completely. However, controlling your spatial environment to be conducive to reprogramming your mind might look as simple as keeping an inspiring talk on your phone to listen to every time you get in the car. Turn your car into a rolling university—especially if you commute and spend anywhere from one to four hours in the car daily. Think about all the people who attend night school in the evening for two hours each week. If you drive two hours daily, you can educate yourself in that time by listening to personal development talks, audio books, inspirational audio, or why not learn a new language? This is one way to control and influence your spatial environment. Listening to soothing and peaceful music can also support a sense of relaxation and peace. It can directly affect your sense of place in your environment.

What if you are at home? What can you control in the spatial environment there? You can control what you watch on television, for example. Do you want the last images you see before bed to be violent or negative? (And this is especially important, because in a few paragraphs I'll introduce a technique you can use at bedtime.) Discipline is essential when controlling the spatial environment. How fast do you want to get into your life masterpiece? If you choose to watch television, choose to watch things that serve your highest interests. When you make choices throughout the day, keep the question "is this moving me toward my life masterpiece?" in mind and let it help you make good choices. Then look around at all the things you can do to create a spatial environment that is conducive to moving you forward and reprogramming your subconscious mind.

Just like we talked about in chapter six, don't forget to control the internal environment by watching what you think and say to yourself. Watch your self-talk and replace negative thoughts in the moment. For example, if you find yourself thinking, "I am broke," replace the thought immediately with a positive one, such as "I am wealthy." Think about all of the ways and areas in your life in which you feel wealthy. For example, you may have excellent health, you may have a group of excellent and supportive friends, or you may have a wealth of ideas and inspirations. There are many different expressions of wealth and abundance! If you are using coupons to pay for things, make sure you are using them in the spirit of gratitude and abundance. Don't sit there cutting coupons and repeating to yourself, "I'm so broke, I have no money." Rather, use the coupon and say "thank you" when you do. Turn saving money into a gratitude practice. When I get a bill for the phone, I say "Thank you!" every time. I thank the company for trusting me enough to provide me the service before I pay the bill. This kind of thankfulness keeps me focused on abundance and gratitude, whereas a response like "Ouch! This bill is high!" only keeps us in negative emotion—predominantly that emotional heavy-hitter, fear.

Another aspect of environment that you can control is what I call the 'incremental environment.' Have you ever been waiting for someone who was running late, and thereby found yourself with an extra fifteen minutes free? What did you do in that time? Instead of being cranky that your friend was late, I suggest you use that time in a productive way. Just like in your car, keep interesting and inspiring audio on your phone perhaps, or a book or a notebook handy. Use the fifteen minutes to develop yourself and continue this work. Don't think that fifteen minutes is not enough time to do anything! Whenever I have to pick someone up from the airport and they are late, I get excited. I get excited because I know that, in those moments while I am waiting, I can listen to or read something that progresses me further along in my personal development. I can continue growing while I'm waiting. You can become your own best project as you take these moments and utilize them with incremental space programming. Every incremental space, every unexpected 'extra' amount of time, can be transformed into a learning opportunity, into a chance to revisit and reconnect with your dreams, goals, and desires.

Now, keeping in mind this aspect of controlling your external environment, let me introduce you to two basic techniques for reprogramming the mind. I want to emphasize basic here: Imagine that reprogramming the mind is like karate. When you learn karate, you learn the basics first, like kata. You don't go straight into breaking boards. So it is with reprogramming the mind. Think of these techniques like the basic building blocks of reprogramming the subconscious. As you begin to use these techniques with regularity, you will start to develop a conditioned response. In essence, we are trying to stretch the muscles of our mind, and do this repeatedly so they take new shape and don't contract back to where they once were. Look at a good guitar player—they can still play the guitar while singing, or talking, or smoking. They are not looking at their fingers; their fingers know where to go. Because they have practiced and practiced, they don't necessarily have to think about where to place their fingers for songs they have played forever. This is where we want to get your mind to: A place where your mind is newly conditioned and reprogrammed for positivity, success, or whatever it is you are moving towards.

So what are we waiting for? Let's get into the techniques!

Recall from chapter one that our brains go through different states throughout the day; generally alpha upon waking up, beta throughout the day, theta when relaxed and heading to sleep, and delta when we are in deep sleep. The first technique is to be done while in the alpha state. How can you access the alpha state? This is the state you are in when you first wake up. Try this tomorrow morning—just wake up and be aware of those first moments of awakening. You might notice you hear the birds outside, or perhaps the sound of their chirping infiltrated the end of your dreams. Before you get up and get out of bed, take a moment in this state and just prop yourself up in your bed. Pick one subject and picture exactly how you want your life to look if that subject—money, a person, amazing health—were in your life. Now, remember that the subconscious cannot differentiate between reality and fantasy, and particularly so while you are in the alpha state. To sequence and secure the desired outcome, picture it while you are in this state. For example, say you want a black Mercedes-Benz. In the morning, just as you are waking up and still in the alpha state, picture this Mercedes-Benz exactly as you want it.

A quick explanation before we go on. When we are talking about reprogramming the subconscious mind, you may read or hear the terms 'associated' and 'disassociated' state. A simple way to distinguish between the two is through the following example. Imagine yourself on a roller coaster and really picture yourself on that roller coaster and seeing it through your eyes. This means you might see the bar, the seat, the view, your legs and hands. This is an associated state. Now, imagine you are on the roller coaster, but you are watching yourself on the roller coaster as if you were in a movie. This is being in a disassociated state.

To really be effective in manifesting your desires in the alpha state, you have to picture what you want from the associated perspective. So, back to the Mercedes. Picture the Mercedes exactly as you want it—and include yourself in it. By using this technique in an associated state, we are emotionalizing the experience. Adding the emotion to the experience is like pouring gas on the fire, and it will instantly accelerate change in the subconscious mind. Remember that the subconscious does not differentiate from fantasy and reality, and seeks to provide that which you call to mind. The subconscious mind is like the seat of our golden ability to attract all of the things we want. To effectively print this car onto your subconscious mind, you need to process the idea through each of your senses. Remember, the subconscious mind understands everything through sight, sound, smell, touch, and taste. Picture the Mercedes and then build on this visual by seeing the car through your own eyes as you walk around it. Then reach out and touch the car as if you are actually there. This generates a tactile response in the alpha state. Picture yourself reaching for the door handle and opening the door of the Mercedes. Sit in the seat and feel the leather. Relax in the seat and call to mind the smell of the leather—this will add an olfactory (smell) response to the visual. Then, imagine you are turning on the music and hearing your favorite song—now we have an audio response to add to the olfactory and visual programming around the Mercedes. While you are relaxing in your bed, picturing all of this, visualize yourself relaxing in the car with the seat reclined. Imagine now that you are starting the car, and feel the anticipation and excitement. Remember—what is expected tends to be realized. Keep going with this visualization as you start the car—the car is fast and exhilarating. Point the car somewhere safe, push the accelerator down, and experience the car fully and completely!

What is happening in an exercise like this—whether you are thinking about a Mercedes, or the love of your life, or a fantastic body—is that these experiences in your mind are creating neural pathways in your subconscious mind, and your subconscious mind cannot differentiate between what is imagined and what is real. Your imagination is the co-pilot to engineering each of the things you wish and dream for.

Try doing this every morning for a minimum of twenty-one days without judgment or analysis. Just do it and hold it loosely, allowing it to happen as it will. Repeating this exercise for twenty-one days will create a new response in your neural pathways. This will in turn initiate an exchange that will create situations and interactions that will eventually bring the Mercedes to you. Everything manifests in circumstances and coincidences—it is always a series of events that brings these things to you.

You can apply this technique if you want a relationship—for instance if you wanted to meet the person you will fall in love with, move the strategy into an associated state and bring all five senses into this state. Bringing the five senses into the associated state then kicks in the reticular activating system. This is when all of a sudden you start to see black Mercedes-Benz cars all over the place, or in this case, prospective mates. Your visual physical sense becomes more aware, your audio sense becomes more aware, all the physical senses are working to bring this car into your life. You'll overhear news about a Mercedes for sale, even. All of this happens because you are using your subconscious mind to connect and integrate with Universal Power. You are tuning your subconscious mind into a state of acquisition, whether you want to acquire a Mercedes-Benz, a lover, or anything else.

The second technique is done at night. This time, you will be accessing the alpha state as you experience it just prior to falling asleep. In this exercise, write out an extremely detailed paragraph outlining all that you wish for. Keep in mind—write out a paragraph for one wish at a time! That is to say, don't write a paragraph for the Mercedes-Benz, AND a lover, AND good health. One at a time, and be precise and specific. So if you are writing your paragraph about the Mercedes, start with "I am going to have" or "I own" (because the subconscious deals in definites) and go from there, "... a black Mercedes E-350, with chrome rims, black leather upholstery, a superb sound system" and so on. Be detailed, definite, and specific. Read your paragraph, out loud, eight times before going to sleep. While you are reading it, picture everything in great detail. Reading it out loud gives you another sensory reinforcement, stimulating the auditory sense. After you have done this, think of one word that sums it up. In the case of my example, the word would be 'Mercedes.' Call to mind this one word, and as you drift off to sleep, repeat that word to yourself. This way, you can suspend analysis and allow the subconscious to do its work. Repeat this exercise for twenty-one days. After twenty-one days, you can move on to the next desire if you like. Stick with one thing at a time—think of your subconscious as a flashlight and you want to focus it like a laser beam on one thing at a time. However, after twenty-one days with one paragraph, move on to the next.

Keep growing in your awareness as you delve deeper into this work. Stay aware of how you talk to yourself, aware of how your external environment affects you, and what happens when you first wake up in the morning and before you fall asleep at night. You can and must control your external environment in order for it to support you in creating change in your internal environment. Take twenty-one days to do the exercises outlined in this chapter and start to notice what shifts. Have no expectations, but pay attention to what you start to see and hear, and the little miracles that come your way that are more in congruence with what you want in the world.

Chapter Twelve: Universal Laws and Rules of the Mind

Many of you may have heard of the twelve Universal Laws. For sure, you will have heard of the Law of Attraction, since it has become wildly popularized through books and film over the last few years. Many of you may have experienced programs, or personal development books, that suggest success through using the Universal Laws. Still others of you may have found that it wasn't that simple, and the Universal Laws were not effective in the practical application you tried. Throughout my years of working in personal development, I have come up with my own Eight Rules of the Mind. What I have observed through implementation of the Eight Rules is this: If you apply my Eight Rules of the Mind with the Universal Laws, you will activate their power and thereby turbocharge your own capability to make manifest all that you desire. Applying the Universal Laws with the Eight Rules of the Mind at a deeper level will serve to amplify their power and effectiveness in your life.

Just like there is a virtually universal way to get in shape, and that is to exercise regularly, so there is a universal way to access the world's abundance. The latter involves knowing and using the Universal Laws. Now, just as there are a million different ways to exercise, and some people believe Crossfit or P90X are the most effective ways of training the body, I believe that combining my Eight Rules of the Mind with the Universal Laws is like doing Crossfit AND P90X daily to get in shape! It's a double whammy of powerful techniques to retrain your subconscious mind.

There are twelve Universal Laws. In brief, these laws are:

1. The Law of Divine Oneness. This law is the foundation of the universal laws, and is about the interconnectedness of everything within the universe. Just as I have mentioned previously how the subconscious mind is the access point to this Universal Power, so this law serves to back up the idea that all energy comes from this place of Universal Power. This law also is about how what we think, say, and do affects everyone and everything around us.

2. The Law of Vibration. This law is about how everything in the universe moves and vibrates. Each thing, each sound, even each thought has its own vibrational frequency. These vibrational frequencies move in spiral patterns. If you take a good close look at some of the beauty of nature, you will start to see these spiral patterns everywhere.

3. The Law of Action. This law is about generating action to support your thoughts and dreams and it must be undertaken to achieve any physical manifestation of thoughts, dreams, or goals. However, this law suggests that once action is taken, this law comes into effect to ensure the dreams and goals come to fruition.

4. The Law of Correspondence. This law is about how the physics, particularly quantum physics, accounts for all the energy, light, vibration, and motion experienced in the physical world and their counterparts in the energetic realm.

5. The Law of Cause and Effect. This law translates simply as, "Every action has a reaction." This law is also commonly matched to the concept of 'karma.' Basically, if you are mean to someone and they are mean to you in return, you are experiencing the Law of Cause and Effect.

6. The Law of Compensation. This law applies the Law of Cause and Effect to allow for abundance to come to those in response to acts of giving, expressions of gratitude, or other charitable action taken. The abundance or gifts that are received come in direct relation with the acts of giving that have occurred. For good or bad, that which you give is returned. When you are angry, you will encounter others who are angry. When you are generous and giving, you will be sure to receive.

7. The Law of Attraction. Simply put, this law states that, "Like attracts Like," whether in our thoughts or our actions. We draw that which we think of to us, like a magnetic attraction. This is the most talked-about and popular of the laws, in use by numerous people in the personal development field to help people manifest their desires.

8. The Law of Perpetual Transmutation of Energy. This law is about the potential we have to change the energy, or vibrational output, in our lives by recognizing that there are higher and lower vibrations. Applying this law along with skilled use of energies and vibrations allows us to shift energy and effect change in our lives. On a practical level, an example of this is how you choose to respond to people that annoy you at work; someone using this law will choose to respond with love and compassion, regardless of the annoyance, knowing that their response will allow them to feel better about the situation, and accepting the fact that they cannot control the people that annoy them.

9. The Law of Relativity. This law reveals that the problems we receive as individuals and in our lifetimes are only as challenging as we need them to be; that we are only ever faced with that which we can handle and ultimately better ourselves for having learned from. This law also invites us to gauge our lives, and perceived problems in our lives, relative to one another.

10. The Law of Polarity. This law works with opposites. All things have an opposite—think of the sun and the moon, black and white, yin and yang. Applying this law on a practical level looks like choosing a positive thought to replace a negative thought to hold in your mind.

11. The Law of Rhythm. This law is about the universal rhythms that guide universal flow, through the seasons, and the human life cycle, for example. Everything is moving to its own rhythm.

12. The Law of Gender. This law is about creation, and the manifestation of all things in the masculine or the feminine.

Many of you have probably already heard of all of these Laws, especially the Law of Attraction. I'm not going to dive too much deeper into each law to explain how to make it work for you. What I am going to do, rather, is outline for you the Eight Rules of the Mind, and then match them up with what I perceive to be the corresponding Universal Law to maximize effectiveness in practice.

Here are the Eight Rules of the Mind:

1. Every thought or idea causes a physical reaction.

2. What is expected tends to be realized.

3. Imagination is more powerful than knowledge when dealing with your own mind or the mind of another.

4. Opposing ideas cannot be held at the same time.

5. Once an idea has been accepted by the subconscious, it remains until replaced by another idea. The longer it has been held, the more opposition there is to replacing it.

6. An emotionally induced symptom tends to cause organic change if persisted in long enough.

7. Each suggestion acted upon creates less opposition to successive suggestion.

8. When dealing with the subconscious mind and its functions, the greater the conscious effort, the less the subconscious response.

Let's look at these rules now within the context of the Universal Laws.

Rule number one: every thought or idea causes a physical reaction. This corresponds to the Universal Law of Cause and Effect. The Law of Cause and Effect reiterates that nothing happens by chance. Every action has a reaction, according to this law. If we take this further and merge it with my rule, which specifies that not only does every action have a reaction, but that every thought or idea causes a physical reaction, we can start to see the truth behind the advice to watch our thoughts. Basically, every thought that passes through your mind, whether generated consciously or subconsciously, will cause a physical reaction. For example, you might think to yourself "I want a new car." You work hard, you earn the money required, you go to the car dealer, you test drive a car, you buy a car, and soon enough, you have your new car. Regardless of how long it took between the thought and the reality of having that new car, the thought of "I want a new car" produced the new physical reality of you in a new car. Now, what if you find yourself suddenly wanting ice cream, without noticing that you had the thought that you want ice cream? Perhaps you watched a commercial or it is a hot day, and something triggered your subconscious mind to provoke that thought. This leads to you buying ice cream. Think back to times in your life when this has happened and you'll notice how every thought led to a physical reaction.

What is important to recognize about this is that the thought comes before the reaction. Pay attention to where you react, particularly when you have reacted without thinking, and chances are you were reacting out of a pattern generated by your subconscious. It makes no difference whether your thoughts are good or bad, but they will generate an effect on the physical body. There is the story of a woman who believed so wholeheartedly that she was pregnant that her hormones actually changed and her body physically manifested the power of that thought and belief. Thoughts are powerful, and this is the bottom line. Thoughts affect our physical reality, regardless from where the thought is generated. It is important to understand this first and foremost as one of the Rules of the Mind, so that you can start to fully grasp the power of the mind, both conscious and subconscious.

The next Rule of the Mind is this: What is expected tends to be realized. This is in line with the Universal Law of Attraction. The Law of Attraction is all about how we create the events that surround us in life. This law suggests that like attracts like; that is, if you are constantly struggling and your mindset is focused on the struggle, then you will only serve to generate more struggle. It also means that if you are focused on the positive and seeing the world as abundant, then you will generate positive thoughts and abundance. The way I see it, with this rule, your thoughts hold expectation and whatever it is you expect, consciously or not, will come to be present in your reality. If you expect to be in poor health, you will be in poor health. If you expect to be wealthy, you will be wealthy. This law is an insidious cancer on the negative, but a powerful force on the positive for those who really get it. The brain responds to images, regardless of whether these images were internally or externally generated. This means there is unlimited potential within each of us to either manifest all the positive things we want, or crash and burn. Do you expect to be in good shape and good health, with a flourishing business and loving, healthy relationships? Do you expect everything that you touch to fail, and a life of pain and misery awaiting you? This is the power within this law. If you expect the doom, you will realize the doom. If you expect goodness, you will receive goodness. Once you reprogram your mind so your subconscious is not keeping you in old patterns that have you expecting what you've perhaps already had for your whole life—misery, misfortune, you name it—then you can step into this law more fully, knowing that what you expect, you realize.

The third Rule of the Mind states that imagination is more powerful than knowledge when dealing with your own mind or the mind of another. This is also congruent with the Law of Attraction, particularly when we consider that the subconscious mind responds to visuals and images. In our world today, where we are literally saturated by images suggesting things to us all day, every day, it is important to continue the work of visualization in order to achieve your dreams. To visualize and imagine what it is you are wanting will help you create it much faster, as this is the language the subconscious mind can respond to. What you watch and the images you take in affect you too, so be mindful about what you choose to look at. When you watch violent TV shows or look at images of things you don't want, your mind is not registering these things as good or bad, but the images are coming in regardless. Selecting, with discernment, the images that you hold in your mind is one of the keys to drawing your dreams closer. Try to shut out or at the very least limit the images and media that do not contribute to your desired 'big picture' result.

While you cannot control every image that is presented to you, it is again important to be aware of the images you hold in your mind. For example, consider the salesman who has a brand new product and a warehouse full of stock and he is excited to sell. There he is, the proverbial 'shingle' hung out, and no one buys anything on his first day of business. Now the salesman has a choice. He could imagine nothing but failure and picture his warehouse closed and locked for good, his sad shingle falling by the wayside. Or, the salesman could imagine wild success, his products flying off the shelves, and not interpret how his first day went as the harbinger of certain doom. Either way, it is in the salesman's control what image he wants to send to his subconscious mind to generate a physical reality. Consider how you respond to the ups and downs of life, and watch what your imagination creates.

The fourth Rule of the Mind is that two opposing ideas cannot be held at the same time. This is linked with the Law of Polarity. The Law of Polarity states that everything has an opposite. Knowing that everything has an opposite, we can then eliminate the negative thoughts we experience by concentrating on positive thoughts in their place. This is a valuable law to understand, because within this concept is the real root of the work of reprogramming your mind. If you catch yourself thinking a negative thought like "I'm so broke," you cannot think "I'm so rich" simultaneously. However, if you catch yourself with the negative thought, and quickly shift to the positive thought, you have in that moment made a conscious choice to hold on to an idea that supports you, not erodes you. If you think about the bouncer at the door of your nightclub, the analogy of the mind used in chapter two, sometimes when your nightclub is occupied with negative thoughts, it feels like a burden. But there are people out there who don't feel this as a burden, because they have repopulated their nightclubs with positive thoughts, knowing that the nightclub cannot entertain both types of thoughts at the same time. Applying this rule in a practical sense requires being aware of your thoughts at all times, and consciously canceling out the negative thoughts to replace positive ones. This means that you can no longer float through your day feeling like you don't know why things are happening like they are. The more present you can become to the thoughts that sabotage you throughout each day, the more you will be able to catch them and replace them with thoughts that lift you.

The next rule of the mind is as follows: Once an idea has been accepted by the subconscious mind, it remains until replaced by another idea. The longer it has been held, the more opposition there is to replacing it. Again, the Law of Polarity is at work through this rule. This is essentially the repopulating of the nightclub. Once you decide to reprogram your mind so that your subconscious mind no longer controls you with its limiting and unsupportive patterns, it will be an effort to replace these thoughts with positive ones. Your subconscious mind will put up a great fight because it believes it knows best and is protecting you. A struggle will be presented. After all, a lot of the patterns running from your subconscious mind were survival mechanisms formed from your childhood to keep you safe and assure your needs were met. You bet it has dug in its heels! However, if it is limiting you in your present life and you know you want to transform your life into the rich and aligned life it could be, then you will have to work day in and day out to reprogram your mind. This is not to say don't do it—far from it. Rather, this is just to allow you to understand that the subconscious mind will give some push-back at the beginning as you repopulate the nightclub. The key point to focus on in this rule is that the subconscious mind accepts ideas from the conscious mind, and that these ideas can be replaced. I am saying that you take this one step deeper in your personal work, and seek to replace these ideas with the right techniques in order to create lasting change at the level required.

Rule of the Mind number six is this: An emotionally induced symptom tends to cause organic change if persisted in long enough. This loosely corresponds with the Law of Perpetual Transmutation of Energy. This Law reminds us that we all have the power to change within us. We can strive to operate from that place of our highest selves and stop operating from ego or limiting identity. If we apply this rule of the mind, backed up by the Law of Perpetual Transmutation of Energy, we can effect change at a profound level in our lives. This rule of the mind invites us to go beyond just thought and get to the emotion behind the thought. For example, think about how you react every time you receive a bill that is more than you were anticipating. For a lot of you, you might react with anxiety or stress, regardless of whether or not you have the funds to pay the bill. Have you wondered where the anxiety or stress have come from? More often than not, the anxiety around paying a bill has nothing to do with the physical work of paying the bill. Even a millionaire could be subject to feeling anxiety when faced with a large bill. The anxiety is the emotion associated with the act of paying bills. Wouldn't it be nice to change that? This rule is an invitation to grow awareness of how you respond emotionally to things. The awareness then gives you access to changing your emotion. You no longer need to default to anxiety if you get present to what is really happening. If you are delighted with your life, it's your daughter's wedding day, your emotional state is genuinely happy and loving, and then you get a bill and feel anxious all of a sudden, what emotion is more authentic? The happy and loving emotions, of course. The anxiety popping up is learned, and not reflective of your present truth in that moment. This is how you know which emotions are coming out of programming in the subconscious mind and which are really real for you in each moment. Chances are, some of the emotions that don't feel so great are ones that you don't even know where they came from. Just like you can work on flipping your negative thoughts into positive thoughts, so with this rule can you work on dispelling emotions that grip and sabotage you, carried over from your subconscious, to make room for actual authentic emotions that serve you. Implementing this rule gets you present to what is actually happening emotionally in each moment, versus what is a manufactured emotion brought up by the subconscious mind.

The next Rule of the Mind states that each suggestion acted upon creates less opposition to successive suggestion. This is reflected in the Law of Rhythm. Everything in the universe has its own rhythm—think of the seasons, or even our own life cycles as humans. As we grow more aligned with the universe, so we see where we can avoid wasting our time on inconsequential or self-sabotaging thoughts and behaviors. As you evolve, and start to suggest new possibilities to your subconscious mind, you will see it only becomes easier over time. As you begin the work of repopulating your nightclub and bringing more positive thoughts into your mind, your subconscious mind will loosen its grip on the long-held thoughts and beliefs, and be more receptive to the new suggestions you are giving it. Recall that the subconscious mind is highly susceptible to suggestion, which is why the reprogramming techniques I am sharing with you are so effective.

Finally, the last Rule of the Mind states that when dealing with the subconscious mind and its functions, the greater the conscious effort, the lesser the subconscious response. This again works along the lines of the Law of Perpetual Transmutation of Energy. Energy is constantly shifting; no matter how stuck we feel, we are actually in a constant state of change. Our cells are repeatedly dying and being born, air is moving in and out of our lungs, our bodies are undertaking hundreds of bodily functions in each moment. As we apply the Rules of the Mind in concert with the Universal Laws, we begin moving out of being programmed human beings whose subconscious minds are running the show and into conscious individuals making choices in real time with full awareness. This is true empowerment. It takes a big, conscious effort to overwrite years of survival programming, patterns, and beliefs that are outdated. It is essential, however, that the conscious effort is guided in the right direction. The conscious mind will redirect the subconscious mind to whatever it is you desire, so it is crucial to redirect the subconscious mind in a positive way.

Applying these Rules of the Mind with the Universal Laws may be the missing link for those of you who have not achieved success in changing through using the Universal Laws alone. Just like you can go to the gym and do some weights and some cardio, or you can go to a Crossfit class and get a killer workout, so can you either implement the Universal Laws in your life, or you can merge them with these Rules of the Mind and work on a much deeper level to effect change in your life.

In the next chapter, I will discuss how you can deepen this integration even further by connecting with the power of emotional expectation. As you apply the Rules of the Mind with the Universal Laws, it is important to include emotion and the role it plays in the operations of your subconscious mind. The blending of the Universal Laws, the Rules of the Mind, and the power of emotional expectation are what will give you true liftoff into taking charge of your life—and turning it into a masterpiece.

Chapter Thirteen: The Power of Emotional Expectation

By now as you are reading this book, you are beginning to put the pieces together. You may be starting to see even in your own life how your thoughts create your reality. You may be more aware of the Universal Laws and have even started noticing them in action in your daily life. You may have started using the techniques for adjusting your mind that I outlined in chapter eleven. Now, have you started noticing your emotions? In this chapter, I want to really dive deep into just how powerful emotional expectation is, especially when trying to reprogram your subconscious mind.

The power of emotional expectation is tremendous. Most of you may be aware of the work of Ivan Pavlov, Nobel Laureate in 1904. Pavlov studied digestive processes of animals, although his work became more famously known after he observed dogs salivating at the sound of a buzzer that went off when food was to be served to them. The dogs knew that food was related to the sound of the buzzer—they had the expectation that they would be fed, and thus salivated before the food even arrived.

We are not that much different than Pavlov's dogs when it comes to expectation and response. It has been proven that when we are engaged in expecting good things, our dopamine levels rise. When we have an expectation that is unmet, our dopamine levels decrease and the disappointment felt can sometimes be surprisingly strong. We are motivated to expect greater things in life, and, despite what we believe, it is possible that the act of expecting is in itself the best part, even better than the act of receiving what it is that we expect.

The subconscious mind is a future-pacing mechanism. What I mean by this is that it is accentuated and accelerated by growth within an individual. Many people want to grow without having to struggle. They want to become the butterfly, while skipping the caterpillar process that involves bursting out of the cocoon. The human mind is actually sparked through the catalyst of struggle. There is nothing wrong with struggle. Struggle becomes a reward, becomes an emotionalized arrival of the destination. When you are watching a movie, notice what scenes arouse your emotional responses. They are usually the scenes where the character is facing struggle or has accomplished something incredible. When you observe the way people behave, you often have an emotional reaction, or your observations are rooted in emotion. The subconscious operates and perpetuates based on emotion. Most people don't gamble for money, they actually gamble to feel the excitement of winning.

Most people are engaged with the process of pursuit. Consider the actions of a hunter. Let's say this particular hunter has been struggling with the weather and having to sit in the woods for hours. Why does he do this? He does this for the thrill he feels in the pursuit of his trophy. The human mind likes the reward. Rather than enjoying traveling in a well-lit tunnel, the mind really likes the light at the *end* of the tunnel. It has been said many times that the weak and the strong, the rich and the poor, the well-informed and the less informed are always changing places. What this means is that people are either becoming complacent where someone else is willing to struggle, or someone is becoming lethargic while someone else is engaged in growing themselves. Even a plant must push its way to the surface of the earth. In order for a human being to encompass and integrate these principles of the subconscious mind, you must go through a learning period, must master the craft, must sharpen the sword, must be able to go into that internal battle with the expectations of coming out a winner. You most certainly can do that. Each and every one of you reading this book can do that. You must look for the realistic way, however, and not the easy way.

The people that look for the easy way in life are the 'have-nots.' They are always looking for the easy way. Is it possible to invent an easier way to do something, yes, but the process of invention is the struggle. The inventor had to risk their money, or their time, without guarantee of the outcome. This is the risk-reward ratio. So, of course you can make it easier to travel and easier to do many different things in your life. The people who have more ease in their lives have this because it was precipitated by a struggle and a risk. Risk is a form of struggle. When you go to the gym to build muscle, it is a struggle to lift the weight. When you have to overcome the fear of approaching someone of the opposite sex, it is a struggle, but the reward could be a life-long marriage to your soulmate. When you are creating a new business, it is a risk because you could lose money, or time. There is no guarantee. Struggle is what the subconscious integrated into an expectation an emotional expectation of victory. So therein lies your powerhouse, your storehouse of power within your mind is directly related to your expectation. What is expected tends to be realized.

When the expectation of victory is precipitated by struggle, it becomes emotionalized. Inertia is either going to pull you forward or set you back. You're either going to gain or lose ground. If you want to improve something, then you have to start moving towards something else. You have to start reaching up. If you want a higher income, you have to stretch up. If you want more muscles, you have to stretch up. This is how growth works and how people grow from a core being into a being of design. Illness removed, everyone can live a life, but they live life by circumstance, not by design, because they move away from any form of struggle. Other people realize that engaging in the struggles actually builds strength, whether this is in the gym, or through entrepreneurship, or making money, or with relationships. Strength builds because the subconscious mind becomes emotionally amplified with the expectation of victory that comes at the end of struggle. A winner knows they've won before they've even entered the race. What we expect, we receive. This is true all around us, whether we are using this for the purposes of manifesting a successful business, a bigger bank account, or a loving relationship.

As another example, consider how we treat each other as humans. How many different beliefs and stereotypes affect our expectations of each other every day, without your even being aware of it? Think of the bad kid in school—always misbehaving, getting into trouble. What happened to that kid? His teachers expected he would misbehave and get into trouble. So, he misbehaved and got into trouble. It is a never-ending cycle that perpetuates itself. His subconscious mind was programmed with a belief that he would not be successful and his expectation was aligned with this.

We have expectations all the time about everything, from how the day should unravel to expecting our partners to be home on time for dinner. We have expectations of others and ourselves, expectations about how to show up with each other, or of what we are really capable of. Much of our experiences are shaped by our expectations and much of these expectations are generated by our subconscious minds, without our even being aware of them.

This is all part of the big E expectation, expectation in a general sense. What I really want to focus on in this chapter is the power of emotional expectation in creating your life masterpiece. We go through life with expectations of ourselves and others, or of the things we want to do, or how we want to live and we don't pay nearly enough attention to the power these expectations really have. When you have an expectation coupled with a strong emotion, you are creating that expectation in your experience of reality. This is powerful stuff!

Recall from chapter twelve the rule of the mind that states, "What is expected comes to be realized." When you really integrate this concept, you will start to pay close attention to what you say, what you think, what expectations you hold for yourself and others in terms of behavior. When you really understand the power that the mind and emotion working together yield for you, with the right action, things can start to change—and quickly—in your life.

How do you talk to yourself in the day? Let's say you are up for a big promotion at work—how do you prepare yourself in the morning you are due to hear the news? Do you look in the mirror, hopeless, and tell yourself you won't get it? Or do you look in the mirror with full knowing that the promotion is yours, and tell your reflection the same? If you expect to be passed by for this promotion, you will be. And you will continue to be, until you recognize that your expectation is creating your reality.

What if you are in a relationship that suddenly starts heading towards the finish line? Did you expect that relationship to go awry? Sure, sometimes we really are blindsided by life and what it hands us. Most of the time, however, we have expectations hiding in our subconscious minds that express themselves through our reality.

What is happening with your thoughts, and your inner dialogue, is that you are putting orders into the subconscious mind with each thought. The subconscious mind cannot differentiate between reality and imagination, and it wants to provide you with what you want. So if you want good health, you cannot go around thinking or saying "I'm sick" all the time. Think about times you do this in your life. It is incredibly common among so many people to walk around all day thinking either "I'm so broke," "I'm so tired," or any other limiting thought. Until you really start paying attention to the thoughts that affect you the most, you are running stories out of your subconscious that you are probably not even aware of!

I have an exercise I like to do in my seminars where I will invite a participant onto the stage and ask him or her to repeat after me. Then the phrase I give them is usually along the lines of "I have a fatal disease." Nine times out of ten, no one wants to repeat this phrase. Why? Because they know— or at least, they may have just learned that night—that what they expect becomes reality. Saying "I have a fatal disease" is scary because it tells your subconscious mind you have a fatal disease and you worry you might contract a fatal disease. What these people don't realize, however, is that all too often I see them leave my seminar and head home for the evening, all the while telling themselves they are broke, they are going to be single forever, they are not lovable, they are tired, they feel unwell... you name it! You have to get clear on what you are thinking and what thoughts and messages are going to your subconscious mind—it's that simple.

It is that simple, yes, but it still takes a lot of work. It requires diligence and awareness to stay on top of your thoughts. Of course, you can't possibly gauge every single thought that comes through your mind, but you can at least detect the habitual thoughts and thought patterns that are like your old friends. You must know what those are. Do you have a refrain you repeat daily without thinking about it? Look around you—how you are living right now is a good indication of how you are thinking. Are your finances in order? Are you wealthy or just getting by? Is your relationship healthy? Is your body healthy? How do you respond when emotions get hold of you? Are you resilient?

It's not enough to dream about a big yacht and think that it will simply come to you. If you believe that, you may need to go back to chapter one and read again all of the concepts we have discussed so far. It is the awareness of what you are thinking, catching yourself in the act of thinking, and replacing those thoughts with what you really want that is the work required. Yes—it's work. Back up thought replacement with emotion and then you will begin to see the changes you wish to see in your life.

The subconscious mind thinks in images, and cannot hear a negative, so let that inform your first foray into redirecting your thoughts to the positive. When you are thinking about what you want, or expecting what you want, you cannot phrase it as "I don't want __." You must phrase the thought in the affirmative, so that the subconscious mind receives a very clear message. Your current thought patterns are deeply entrenched within your neural networks, and they only continue to be reinforced when you repeat them again and again daily. The good news is that you can change your thought patterns. To be successful, you must invest in using your time to practice diligently.

What could be more enjoyable, however, than the work involved in reorganizing your thought patterns to send desirable thoughts to your subconscious mind? These desirable thoughts then become your desirable life, and won't that make it all worthwhile? At some point in your life, you have to put the books down, go to a seminar or workshop where you can practice experientially, and begin to put everything you have learned into action on a daily basis. You can start with recognizing the power of emotional expectation.

The subconscious mind is the center for accessing the Universal Power within you. As your desire heightens emotionally, there will come a point when the emotional intensity is what acts to move matter and manifest that which you desire. Once you get your thoughts on track, backing them up with strong emotional intensity is what really lights the fire of creation.

Rearrange your thoughts so they are positive—this is essential. The emotional aspect is also essential, however. It is not enough to just be aware of your thoughts and rephrase them in a positive way if you are really adamant about achieving your dreams and the life you desire. You must back up the positive thoughts with strong emotion of expectation. Remember that concept of thinking like a winner. The expectation will release the dopamine, which will contribute to your feeling good throughout the process. The underlying emotion behind the thought propels the thought into creation.

How do you ensure that the underlying emotion will be a positive one? This is the tricky part. Think back to a time in your life when you felt confident, or happy. Now think back to a time in your life when you felt sad. What happens with many people is they find they are unable to get over things like divorce, or loss, or other challenges, because they continue to revisit the sadness or negative emotion that was present during the event. I want to show you how you can call up your past emotions and use them for good, to propel your life forward in a positive way. The insidious cognitive cancer that affects all of us happens when we set up the expectation and emotionalize the thought out of our past experiences, only we use negative emotions. Through this practice, we are allowing our past to become the designer of our future, so it is vital that we choose only those positive emotions from our past.

Emotions can be borrowed from our past experiences and applied to our current experiences. Imagine you are a tennis player. You expected to win your last match, you did win your last match, and the win provided you with a positive emotion and confidence. Now, to access that emotion and use it to your advantage, take a moment to quiet your mind. Recall the alpha state techniques I explained in chapter eleven, and do this when you are in a similar state. Allow yourself to access a positive emotion from your past. For example, the time you wanted to date that girl and you did, or the time you won your baseball game, or the time you wanted to get that promotion and you did. With this exercise, we are going to borrow the emotion from the past, and future-pace it into the present. In your mind's eye, create a horizontal line and picture that line so that right in front of you is the present moment. Now picture a small circle on the line. Move the circle to the left, as if you are moving a volume control on a stereo, and access an emotion attached to a word. Words like confidence, love, joy; words that are positive and meaningful to you. Now, picture your mind going back perhaps one month, perhaps one year, perhaps two years, or more. Take yourself back in time in your mind's eye and when you get to an event where you were confident, in love, joyful, or whatever word you chose, bask in that moment. Become emotionally aware of how you felt. Memory is infallible, and the subconscious mind never forgets anything, so allow it to do its work, and access that emotion, the feelings generated from the positive experience.

Now that you feel that emotion, let's say it's confidence, take that confidence and in your mind's eye put it in the little circle on your line. Supercharge the circle with your energetics of confidence and the feelings of confidence. Begin to slide the circle now, filled with your confidence, to the right until it lands in front of you again—in the present moment. Take that little circle, filled and infused with confidence, and pull it into your head. This is a technique known as an 'absorption protocol.' Essentially, what you will have done is installed confidence in the present by borrowing confidence from the past. This is a very powerful and effective way to emotionalize your thoughts and attract what you want to you in your life.

That's not all, however! Now let's do some future pacing. Imagine a time in the future where you want to succeed. Maybe you have a golf game coming up that you hope to win. You can imagine the event in the future, and take that same circle infused with your confidence and move it along the line to the right of your present moment, and energetically charge the event. You are now anchoring in your subconscious the confidence from the past and inserting it into your present.

Emotion is energy, and energy has no lifespan; it is only transformed. By pushing this emotion into your future, when you go to your golf game, you will now have an elevated sense of confidence. Essentially, we are borrowing our emotions from the past to fuel our expectation. We can craft the future by maximizing the present through this technique.

Let's do it again. Put that little circle back on the line, close your eyes, and see that circle at the present moment. Move that circle to the left until you access a past point in time where you experienced the emotion of love. Bask in the emotion, how good it felt, how inviting. Infuse that little circle with the remembered emotion, and travel it back along the line to present time. Move the circle perhaps a little into the future, and think about the person you have a crush on, or even a place or thing you want to love and look forward to loving. Borrow the emotion, move it into the future and anchor that emotion to a future event.

Simply put, the thoughts are like a match. The intention then is what strikes the match, and the emotion is like adding gasoline to that struck match that turns the spark of thought into an inferno of results. This is the most basic formula when understanding the power of emotional expectation in creating the life you dream of and attracting all that you seek.

There is a caveat, of course. You must control your emotions. Once you see how emotion hangs on to people, places, locations, and events, you must learn to spot when you have anchored negative emotions to an experience.

Anchoring negative emotions to an experience is like polluting a beautiful, pristine lake.

What do I mean by anchoring negative emotions to experiences? Do you get into your car and feel angry, regardless of the day or what's happening? This is a common example. What is happening here is that you had an experience in your car, being stuck in traffic or in an accident or something that made you angry, and you now feel that anger every time you get in the car. Do you hate your job? Whatever may have happened to you at work may have left the emotion of hate towards the workplace and anchored it to your job, so that you always feel that emotion when you think of work. To change this, simply use the technique I outlined above again, and move the little circle all the way to the left until you access something about that job that brought you happiness or joy. Move that happiness back over on the line to your present. Using thought dilution, you can make the emotion and thought less omnipotent. Nothing is omnipotent! With this process, you can clean your slate so you can quantum leap your thought processes and get to the creation of your reality faster.

It might be difficult to really concentrate and call upon emotion when you begin using this technique in your life; however, stick with it. The addition of the emotional expectation makes all of your thoughts real in a deeper way to the subconscious mind, and this is where the action is. Building upon all of the techniques explained so far in the book, the next chapter will explain how you can amplify the power even more to effect change in the subconscious mind, and therefore your reality.

Chapter Fourteen: Amplifying the Power

The difference in our quality of life is not about our capability, background, or education. Human beings—that means you—are all capable of achieving incredible results, and yet sadly only a few seem to understand this.

What people WILL do is very different from what people CAN do.

I want to challenge you right now to start using your WILL muscle, instead of your TRY muscle, which is probably overdeveloped anyhow. I challenge you to start exercising your inborn human power, which is your birthright as a member of the human race, your ability to act based on the choice and free will that every human has in equal measure. Frankly, this means that if it has been achieved, then there is no reason on earth why you cannot achieve it. And beyond that, if it can be imagined, then there is also very little reason why you cannot achieve it. As a matter of fact, your subconscious mind will rarely imagine something that you are not capable of. That is the difference between desires and fantasies. It's true. There are no excuses anymore. If you are reading this and you are human being, then you have the ability to take action and to produce results. We are made of all the same matter that the universe is made of, and the universe wants to continue to expand and create upon itself through us.

This ability that I'm talking about is not something I can give you. Why? Because you already have it. You were born!

Great. Now I challenge you to go out and take back what is rightfully yours.

Hopefully, something is now awakened within you in two ways. One, by igniting your desire and two, by showing you some simple systematic strategies on how you can get greater results out of yourself on a daily basis.

When the intention is to magnify the power, one of the biggest principles and one of the most effective techniques you can use is objective focus. Objective focus does not mean being objectively removed, it means focusing on your objective. What happens to an average person is that they are focused on the present chaos in their life in many cases, or the responsibilities, or the ups and downs of the emotional roller coaster that everybody deals with. A successful person, regardless of whether that means successful in their relationships, finances, or health, is focused on the end objective. The more they stay in tune, in touch, and in synchronicity with that objective on a subconscious level, the more they are drawn to it, the stronger their pull, and the stronger the reciprocity that the universe creates for that pull.

Let me give you an example. Let's say you took a magnet and you put it close to a piece of steel or iron. You would have the maximum pull if it stays close to the objective, or the objective in this case that you're looking to do. The farther you pull that magnet away from the objective, the weaker the draw becomes. So the farther you're pulled away from your objective, or your goal, then the weaker or more diluted the subconscious energy and its ability to create or co-create the objective becomes. Now, in theory this principle sounds simple. That being said, it must be merged together with concentration and intention. To magnify what the subconscious is capable of doing, the objective must be in close proximity in the mind at all times. That means you must eliminate or significantly reduce distraction. The more distracted you are, the more the magnet re-orients in another direction and it loses the pull to the original objective or object.

When you are engaged in focused concentration, you're aligning all of your internal powers—mental, physical, and emotional—with what it is that you want. In my personal opinion, we see a dilution of this force now more than ever before in society because of the ability to become so easily distracted by so many different things. Take a look at the people that have set their focus intently on something specific. They create that focus and that objective, and they stay focused on it. If you look for people that are entrepreneurs, for instance, successful entrepreneurs eat, breathe, and sleep their ideas, even if they are parents, even if they have two jobs, even if they have a health condition. They still remain intently focused mentally, and we're talking about the mind here, the subconscious mind. These people retain mental focus, in some cases 24/7. It does not mean that they discard their responsibilities, or their children, or their families, or their spirituality, or their health. It means that—and forgive the cliche—if the objective is out of (mental) 'sight,' it is out of mind. If it's out of mind, then you've diluted the objective focus and the objective concentration that's required to hit that goal. Using this analogy with yourself all the time, asking yourself, "Are you keeping the magnetic poles close to your objective?" keeps your objective present and allows you to monitor your level of focus. You'll also know right away if you're diluting your objective by moving your focus away from that.

I have acquaintances and friends that are professional athletes. One of these friends is a cyclist. He is extremely successful at racing bicycles. If you were to walk into his home, you would see pictures of him racing on the walls. There are bicycle magazines on the coffee table. There are pictures of his bike logo on the wall. He eats, breathes, and lives his career as a cyclist. Even though he is a single father, even though he suffers from health issues, he is still intently focused on success, and that's why he's a champion in what he does. Conversely, I'll go into people's homes, people that claim that they are entrepreneurs who are focused on their endeavors, and I could have a search warrant and I still would not be able to find what it is they do, or what it is they're even into! If you're not into what it is that you are doing, then you're distracted or diluted from what you're doing. Regardless, if you're into health, you're into health. You get yourself to the gym, no matter what. You do that juicing, no matter what. You buy those supplements, no matter what they cost. You are into health, and your actions and your environment reflect this. If you are into success, you are into success and if the vehicle to get you there is an entrepreneurial endeavor, you eat, breathe, and live it. You are a person that is passionate about what you're doing. So many times the people are focused on the present moment only. Don't confuse that with being in the now or mindfulness; I'm talking about being so polluted psychologically and subconsciously with the present moment that they lose sight of the objective—which is never in the present moment. The objective is always in a future moment.

You have to learn to create excitation and anticipation along with objective focus by getting excited about what is yet to come. That's an entrepreneurial trait that has created the greatest and most successful entrepreneurs. They have the innate ability to focus on what is not there yet. Think about entrepreneurs in the desert in Nevada way back in the day. Some people saw the desert, other people saw Las Vegas. They were all staring at the same empty desert. One person was in the now, looking at the desert with the inability to focus on an objective. Another person, in their mind, in their subconscious mind, was creating Las Vegas out of their ability to magnetically draw to an objective that is not yet physically in front of them. Remember that while you are living in your current reality, you can use the subconscious mind to create objective focus and a magnetic draw and a propulsion to whatever your desired end result is.

When most of us think of success or failure, we tend to think of these monumental things. Failure is not an overnight thing, and neither is success. Just what is success? Some people describe it in terms of achievements, like those we list on our resumes. Success is different for everyone. Some people may describe it as a feeling. It is problematic for you to make it a goal to achieve a feeling for something that is difficult to define. Many programs attempt to do that and they use motivation to give you that temporary feeling of success. But it doesn't last.

The truth is that success is actually wrapped up in failure. What I mean by that is that success is simply a string of failures all going in the same purposeful direction. That's right. If you want to find success, you have to look inside a failure. In other words, if you want to be more successful than the next person, you simply have to be willing to experience more failure, but not just any failure. You must be willing to take specific actions, based on specific decisions, fail most of the time, keep going, perhaps with a new strategy, experience more failures, and eventually you will succeed. If this sounds painful, then I want you to think for a moment about what true failure actually is.

True failure is lifelong failure. It is the failure of inactivity. It's not actually failing at what you *do*, for those are the things that will lead you to success. But when you fail to *do*, you fail to succeed. In failing to do lies the recipe for ultimate failure in life. When you fail to make the calls, when you fail to follow through, when you fail to say "I love you," when you fail to give your all, these are what create the ultimate failure in life. Ultimate failure creates the greatest pain, the feelings we want to avoid at all costs. Now *that* is painful.

Success happens one step at a time. Actually, success happens one failure at a time. It is successfully making the calls and doing it no matter how long it takes for the outcome in the moment. It is successfully getting up and following through. It is successfully making sure that you make that unique contact. It is successfully breaking through the limits that used to stop you.

Success is a combination of all those little things, those little successes that often come disguised as failures, the little things that take place over each day and over your lifetime that eventually create a life that you will have total pride and great joy in knowing that you created.

There are four steps to success when you decide you are ready to amplify the power of the techniques I have shared in this book:

1. Know what you want. It is important for you to know what you want, and for you to know how you want things to turn out. In other words, you must know your outcome before you begin. The first step is to decide what you want out of whatever situation you are currently in. The clearer you are with knowing what you want, the more you will empower your brain to give you the answers.

2. You must use it. In other words, you must get yourself to take action toward your outcome. This means that you must put energy in the right direction, even when you do not know exactly what to do. Many people do not know what to do at first. I will teach you exactly what to do. Some people want to know what happens if they try, and it doesn't work. I can tell you right now, and you will learn why in this book, why nothing you try will ever work. So how do you take action? Decide to. It's not about what you can do. It's about what you will do.

3. Notice your results. It's not enough to take action. You must also pay attention to the results you are getting from your actions. Do your actions always work? No. Remember, success is just a series of failures, but failures with purpose, failures directed at a specific result. You knew what you wanted and you took action; now notice the result.

4. Be flexible and willing to change your approach. You must be willing to make changes and adjustments based on the results of your actions, because flexibility is the key to the system. In other words, if you notice that what you are doing is not working, and you're not getting closer to your goal or even getting further away, instead of feeling like a failure or giving up, sometimes you simply need to change your approach.

Shifting how you view success to begin with, then making use of the tools above, as well as using your will and committing to the techniques outlined in chapter eleven are all ways to amplify the power of this technology. Power comes from concentrating your focus and taking daily action to improve something. Even a 1% improvement today can result in unbelievable change, because 1% per day will give you a 365% difference in the year, because it builds and compounds to create a difference, way beyond anything you can probably imagine right now.

Let me give one more scenario to help guide you as you use these techniques to reprogram your subconscious mind. Imagine five cups on a table, and each one has a label. The first cup you see is labeled "belief." This cup of belief is created by the expectations of your thoughts—do you believe that you are deserving of wealth or great relationships, or do you believe your emotions are under control, for example. That cup of belief is created by the expectancy of thought. Take those thoughts, take the internal communication and pour it into the cup of belief. First you will increase the belief by imagining that you are exactly where you want to be, and you will pour that belief in there. Once that cup is full, you pour it into the next cup. The next cup is labeled "potential." Now the belief in yourself, that unstoppable ally, the belief that you can have more wealth, or great relationships, or emotional control has been poured into the cup of potential.

Now you have mixed unstoppable belief with potential. Mix these and pour them into the third cup, called 'action.' The way you're going to move toward action is by excitation and anticipation of the new you, who you can become, not who you are; where you are going, not where you are right now. You can sit in meditation and pray all day long that you will become a great guitar player. You can sit and stare at the guitar for hours on end, because you believe you will become a great player, you may even have the potential and talent to be a great guitar player, but unless you get up and walk across the room and pick up the guitar and begin to play, you'll never become a great guitar player. Without the component of action, you will never play the guitar. This cup is very imperative. When you fill your cup of action, and execute an action step, this incremental action produces a result. Building on belief and potential, the action taken produces a result and this result is the catalyst for momentum. This might look like your relationship getting better or stagnating, or your business growing or stagnating. Essentially, you are retaining your power, or giving it away.

Pour the cup of action into the next cup, the cup labeled 'results.' Pour the cup of results into the last cup. This cup is called "My Life." You will pour all of those cups into the cup called "My Life" and then you're going to drink it. And the question becomes, are you drinking poison, or are you drinking something that will become part of you and nourish your best self, the best version of you? You're controlling what you're taking in, and you're controlling those cups and your movement forward. You're not changing who you are, you're just becoming a better you; you are still yourself and taking yourself along the journey of life, why not take an improved version of you?

We are born creators, we are part of Universal Power and inherently wired for creation. The thoughts we think are manifest directly into our life experience. There is nothing to fix, nothing to change, only this realization to wake up to in order to truly take hold of the steering wheel of your life.

One of the most powerful principles you can use in creating your own life masterpiece is the power of appreciation and gratitude as applied towards other people, through exhibiting that energy toward another person. Many individuals will exert energy toward their own development or accomplishment. While this is necessary, one of the most powerful forces is reciprocity, and the emotional subconscious Universal Power that will create a reciprocal loop back to you. We have to be aware and give gratitude and appreciation to others on an on-going basis. Everything out there will eventually respond energetically in one way or another, so it is a virtue to be grateful to other people. It is even more powerful to express gratitude because the energy expressed as gratitude moves out into the universe and becomes part of a reciprocal exchange.

Remember the guiding rule that 'like attracts like.' The expression of gratitude works in the same way. Think about it like throwing a boomerang out into the environment, you know that it will come back. Your expression of gratitude and appreciation to another is just like the action of the boomerang. When you put it out into the universe, that energy then comes back to you. Expressing gratitude and appreciation with detachment is also important. The key is to express these sentiments without expecting anything in return. This is paramount. It doesn't matter what your spiritual beliefs are. You may look at the detached action as turning it over to God, or turning it over to the Universe, or simply getting out of your own way. The important piece is that you make the expression of gratitude and appreciation without attaching it to a specific outcome.

Here is an exercise related to this concept that you can try, but first, let me offer you a helpful analogy. Imagine you have found a young bird with a broken wing. You take the bird into your house and you mend its wing with a bandage, you feed the bird with an eyedropper, and you nurse the bird back to health. After a month has passed, the bird is healthy and well. You open the window and set the bird free. Would you expect the bird to return to you and offer repayment for your service? Would you mandate some form of payment for your time nursing the bird? With this mindset, you are actually circumnavigating the universal laws. You must simply allow the universal laws of gratitude and appreciation to permeate your actions as they are expressed through caring for the bird.

Now, here's the exercise: Begin by closing your eyes and picture something that you want. Picture writing it out, using less than five words, with a large black magic marker on a large piece of paper. It could be like this, "I want a brand new Black Mercedes Benz," or it could be "I want a loving relationship." Imagine writing the words out on the paper. Next, rephrase "I want" to "I have." Now we are working with the present tense. Bring to mind the phrase, "I want," then rephrase and restructure the phrase into "I have." Through this method, you are retraining your mind to craft the sentence into a more powerful current reality. Your new phrase would sound like this, "I am driving a brand new black Mercedes," or "I am in a loving relationship."

Next, picture folding that piece of paper, after you have really looked at it in your mind, and picture putting the folded paper inside a beautiful blue balloon that's not yet blown up. Imagine tucking the paper into the balloon that's not yet inflated. Fill that balloon with helium, and see yourself tying a string around the balloon to make sure it stays inflated. Now that you've got your inflated balloon, picture letting the balloon go and watching as that balloon floats away, rising to ten feet, one hundred feet, to one thousand feet. Watch as the balloon floats into the sky until it leaves your sight. Experience what release feels like. What was it like to have what you wanted, a statement representing what it is that you wanted and then to release it?

This is a simplistic example of turning something over to a higher power (God, source, Universal Power, etc.) to help you to get out of your own way. This is an example of relinquishing control because you are only a human being and the Universal Power within your mind synchronized with the omnipotent power of the entire universe can do wonders far beyond what you are capable of as a single human being. The key here is that you must turn the thing you want over and you must relinquish control.

On a daily basis, bring to mind the boomerang analogy; think about spreading seeds, and think about expressing gratitude and appreciation. Picture in your mind the physicality of these actions, the verbal element of these actions (as portrayed through writing), and, most importantly, the energetic aspect of these actions. This is how you harness your emotionalized energy and send it out into the universe (without attachment), so that it can link into and synchronize with the same energetic frequency that already exists in the Universe. It's as though you are energetically tuning into a radio station that is tuned into the exact frequency that enables it to pull that desire back to you. Ninety percent of the population is using this technique in its opposite form. We have talked about this phenomenon at length earlier in this chapter as far as negative expectation happens. These people are actually repelling everything that they want from themselves, instead of pulling the things that they do want towards them. It's far beyond a simple law of attraction, not simply wishing for something, but actively engaging in a process to make it happen. Wishful thinking is just that, wishful thinking. Dynamic engaged, imaginative, and emotionalized thinking is utilizing a power that is within you. It is a tool and therefore it must be picked up and utilized with skill and intention. In this way, you are skillfully using tools the way a good carpenter would, or the way a doctor does. Like a well-practiced musician who uses a guitar to express her art, you too must practice and learn how to apply the technique I shared with you. A hammer and nails are tools that a carpenter uses in his craft. Through practicing these techniques, you will move from being the apprentice, to becoming the journeyman, to becoming the professional.

You can become your own professional, and an expert professional at that, with your own mind. When you accomplish this ability to bring your desires into reality, it will become one of the most engaging attributes that you have. It will become one of the most exciting things available to you to work with daily. This technique will become a new ally, a new friend, a new confidante, one that accompanies you everywhere you go, just like your own best friend or your very own cheerleader. The ability to redefine and re-craft your life the way that you want it is available to you. I've seen thousands of people use these techniques and completely transform their circumstances, regardless of their socioeconomic situations, their physical prowess, their looks, their charisma. I've seen them begin in one place and progress just by understanding how to acquire, utilize, assimilate, and apply the power that you are learning right now. To review, make sure that you understand that gratitude and appreciation make other people feel good, which is an excellent contribution to society. Gratitude and appreciation also create a reciprocal energetic response as I explained previously, just like a boomerang, so as you move closer and closer to your objectives and goals, you will feel great too.

Part 4: Life by Design

Chapter Fifteen: Health and healing

I am certain we can all agree that we all want to enjoy a life of good health. What is the point of wanting wealth, time, and great relationships if we don't have good health and vitality to enjoy all these things? By using the techniques I have outlined in part three, you can begin to take advantage of the Universal Power you have access to through your subconscious mind to cultivate true health and wellness. Regardless of what you may believe is responsible for your physical health and well-being, if you have read the book this far, you are aware that you have more power than you think. Realizing that your thoughts create your reality, and that your thoughts are generated from the subconscious mind, which is also your access point to Universal Power, you can now carefully construct thoughts that support your being in good health.

While there is certainly evidence linking our mental and emotional health to the creation of disease in the body, I don't want you to think I am 'blaming the victim' here by suggesting that people with disease have thought themselves into it. I acknowledge that there are several other factors that come into play, and human physiology is indeed a complicated thing. However, there are also numerous accounts of people who have experienced spontaneous healing, and a wealth of evidence pointing to the power of positive thinking when it comes to recovering from illnesses both minor and major. Positive thinking is the natural result when you come to understand that your thoughts affect your life, you become aware of the power of your thoughts, and begin to actively choose which thoughts to hold in your mind. Moving from a place of being a victim of your thoughts into a place of being in control of your thoughts. Let me put that another way; you can never truly control your thoughts. Your thoughts will forever come and go, like waves in the ocean. But with the awareness that the concepts in this book strive to bring you to, you can notice which thoughts come up to support you, and which thoughts do not support you. You can begin to pinpoint which thoughts come up that are just old, limiting beliefs imprinted upon you without your conscious choosing, and you can choose to let those thoughts go, rather than engage in holding them in your mind in those moments.

When it comes to healing, regardless of the nature of the ailment, the practice of holding positive thoughts is invaluable. Some people might recommend using positive, healing affirmations that you can switch to thinking the minute a negative thought enters your mind. While this is effective, to me it is not always enough. Powerfully visualizing your well body, and emotionalizing the vision (along the lines of the techniques shared in chapter thirteen) will take your healing to a deeper level by bringing it into the subconscious mind. While affirmations work, absolutely, on the mental plane, using visualization and emotionalization have profound results, because they access the subconscious mind and therefore now reach across the physical, mental, emotional, and spiritual planes.

I encourage you to consider working in this area regardless of whether you are already well or are suffering from any ailment, however minor. Growing the muscle of expecting good health will serve you in the event that you do experience health issues in your life. It's just like taking care of your car on a regular basis; you give your car an oil change every three months, right? Beyond eating right and exercising, consider using these techniques to boost your health and well-being as a way of giving your health the same kind of routine maintenance you might give your car.

When you are in the throes of being acutely challenged by health issues, however, you often become open to many different healing modalities that you may not have been otherwise open to. For the most part, we have been raised in an allopathic society. Utilizing self-healing modalities is ever increasing, even though it's certainly been around for a long time. Using self-healing tools invite you to truly engage in your core beliefs around health and healing. It's easy to say you believe in something but, from a subconscious level, if you *truly* believe in it, then it truly creates organic change. In the human body, I've seen people that have had profound changes in their health, simply by adopting strategies of the mind, strategies that became repetitive programming so that the subconscious mind had the ability to expand upon and create that state of health. For instance, if you want something to become your outcome, then you focus on it as if it already is. For example, let's say someone is suffering from a disease. If you say to yourself, "I want this disease to go away, I want this disease to go away, I want this disease to go away" you are just re-affirming the existence of the disease. Your repetition of the word "disease" is only emphasizing its existence in your subconscious mind. The subconscious mind creates an emotionalized imagery to reinforce the existence of the disease and, even worse, the expansion of the unwanted disease.

If you have the ability and the knowledge to focus on what you want, you're not discarding your reality, what you're doing is creating a new reality based on the outcome you seek. Let's say you have a skin condition. To say day in and day out that you want the skin condition to go away is to reaffirm its existence, and now this reaffirmation is accompanied by imagery and emotion. This will yield the opposite result of that which you seek. If instead you were to say, "I have perfect skin," and embed this suggestion along with visual imagery and emotion, the subconscious mind then goes to work, as if an order was placed into a computer, and over time it will produce the perfect skin that you want.

I remember having a woman come to me for help as she was suffering from a 'syndrome.' It seems as though nowadays we have a lot of things that are labeled as a syndrome. A syndrome is basically when the medical community is unable to determine what is happening, there is an unknown cause, or an unknown reason, or an unknown diagnosis in general, so it is thrown into the syndrome category. We all have a multitude of reasons as to the cause of most organic illnesses, such as environmental toxins. However, when people begin to suffer with a syndrome, they are usually experiencing a drastic change from their normal state of health. They become fixated or focused on their ill health, and even though they are focused on it in a positive way, in that they may be proactive in finding a solution, that action in and of itself reinforces the state that they are in, which is a state of ill health. They repeat phrases such as, "I am sick, I must get rid of this, I don't want to feel like this, this (illness) is no good," or, "What happened to me? How do I get over this?" The reinforcement of the very illness or syndrome that they have compounds it and creates an ongoing, indefinite syndrome.

I've found the same scenarios in many people with whom I've worked, and I'll give you an example of one particular situation. A client named Karen came to see me when she was suffering from one of these syndromes. This was at a time when I was accepting select private clients. Karen came to me because she had been to several physicians and other healers in alternative modalities and no one could discern what was wrong with her. Routine tests taken by Karen were shown to be 'normal,' yet she was still experiencing symptoms of malaise, foggy brain, and fatigue, basically all of the vague symptoms that seem so common these days.

I put her into a deep state of hypnosis as we began our session. First, however, I made sure to detach any form of ego gratification she may be seeking from being ill, just in case there was one present. Just for clarification, what I mean when I say "detach from ego gratification" is that some people will unconsciously seek attention by being ill and seek especially to receive the empathy and compassion of others through their being sick. This is not overly common, but I have seen it occur in some cases. When I engage in hypnosis with a client for the purposes of physical healing, I always want to make sure there is a detachment from that core need so that the syndrome doesn't expand based on that core need or its attachment to the ego.

Once I had induced Karen into deep hypnosis, I wanted to identify her desired outcome. It's not enough just to say, "I'm healthy" because that can be entirely subjective. I wanted to be very specific about how Karen wanted her health to be. How did she really want to *feel*? Using descriptive terms emotionalizes those terms, and then we can implant them into the neural pathways of the subconscious mind. By doing so, we access the mechanism that is working internally, 24/7, to create the state that she desires. Of course, by no means is this an alternative or an option to be used exclusive of medical care, however, it can be a complementary treatment. This is because, in a general sense, the medical community will address the presenting physical symptoms, and the hypnosis will address the emotional and mental barriers to healing. In many cases, a syndrome is perpetuated mentally from the stress that it causes. If you are completely stressed about experiencing the syndrome, that stress can produce an organic response in the body and even create a less favorable syndrome than just the syndrome itself.

We all understand how frustrating it can be to have an illness from which you are not recovering quickly. By integrating strategies with the subconscious, Karen was able to alleviate the vast majority of her symptoms—symptoms which the medical community did not perceive as life-threatening, although they were still stumped as to how they could treat these symptoms effectively. Together, Karen and I discovered that it was her mental state perpetuating a physiological condition that caused her to be stuck in this syndrome for two years. Once we were able to reprogram the subconscious mind and get her mental state out of that situation and detach any need for compassion, recognition, or validation, she saw the clouds lift. Progressively, over the next two to three months, Karen saw her health improve and even return to normal. Never underestimate the power that you have within you to create organic change in your own body.

We have the physical capability to keep our bodies functioning perfectly, yet mentally we run all over the place. What you think, you create. Believe it to be true, and it is true. You have access to Universal Power within you, through your subconscious mind, and therefore you have infinite support in creating the health you desire. The subconscious mind responds to visuals and emotion, and also gets rewired through repetition. If you are feeling unwell, or live in fear of attracting serious disease or illness in your life, let this book be an invitation to you to check in with your thoughts and your beliefs. Your deep-seated beliefs around illness, those stored in your subconscious that I remind you may not even have been yours to begin with but were taught to you when your mind was impressionable, these beliefs will inform your view of health and your state of health throughout your life. You can work to uncover and eradicate these beliefs. You can also pay close attention to your mind and your thoughts, so that you can choose to hold positive thoughts around your health. The next time you are actually ill, say with a cold or the flu, common illnesses that we all get from time to time, I encourage you to watch your thoughts closely. Did you start thinking, "Ugh, I feel terrible," before or after you physically noticed that scratch in your throat or your temperature rise? It is never too late to switch your self-talk from that of, "I'm so sick!" to statements like, "I am well again." And the more you can attach belief and a positive emotion and a visual to your statement of wellness, the more the subconscious mind will work to get you well.

This is an infinitely powerful tool you have access to when it comes to your health. Harness that Universal Power and use it to support you to stay strong and healthy. Good health means good energy, which translates into vitality. With good health, good energy, and vitality, you can be more effective in your work and your relationships. Consider good health as the foundation of your life masterpiece, because without it, all the riches in the world will be useless for you. See yourself well, feel yourself well, and commit to taking action to being well in your life. This means staying on track with a diet and exercise regime that is authentic and congruent for you, along with working with whatever medical advisor in whatever modality you prefer, whether you regularly see your physician or prefer to work with a naturopath, and, possibly most important of all, keeping a positive mental and emotional image and belief that you are a healthy and well person present in your conscious and subconscious minds at all times.

Chapter Sixteen: The Art of People

An essential element to our lives as humans is relationship. As the three chapters in this part suggest, the three primary motivations that I see in people who come to me to learn this work are better health, better relationships, and, of course, more money. This chapter will focus on relationships. Indeed, there is no more fundamental and integral aspect to our human experience than the relationships in our lives. Relationships can make us or break us, and even the most introverted hermit still needs connection and relationship in his life.

One could say that all life is relationship. Indeed, relationships really are a life force for us. Especially those we think of as 'love' relationships. Why else would there be so many books, poems, movies, and songs written about love? Love dominates the airwaves and culture across all media. People perk up when they are invited to talk about love—think of anytime you ever asked a couple how they met, and more often than not they were delighted to share the tale.

It is precisely because love relationships play such a profound role in the collective psyche and have taken on a monumental importance that for some people it is all they long for. What is important to recognize is that all of the relationships we have in life need to stay healthy. By healthy, I mean the relationships must operate as the two-way street they are, with equal giving and receiving taking place. They must be open, loving, and fulfill the needs of both parties involved. We must keep all of our relationships in balance, as well. The predominant love relationship, while absolutely guaranteed to need time and energy, cannot just take over. Your relationships with your kids, your co-workers, your friends, your extended family, and, crucially, yourself all need just as much attention and nurturing if you want to truly live an aligned and healthy life.

We interact with people so much on a daily basis, yet so many of our interactions take place with no thought or conscious awareness in the moment. Do you really pay attention to the barista serving your coffee in the morning? Have you ever engaged in conversation with the human scanning and ringing up your groceries? Chances are some days you don't even make eye contact with these people. If you are interested in deepening your experience of your life, and cultivating the richest relationships you can, you will start to extend your relationship awareness beyond the walls of your home. Relationship starts with yourself, and expands to include everyone with whom you interact. Every human you interact with is essentially engaging in a relationship with you, even if it is only for one moment your entire lives. As you start to live with more awareness overall in your life, you will start to pay much closer attention to your relationships and how to develop and nurture them so the best in both parties is able to shine forth.

Thus, the power of the mind is synchronized with the power of awareness. People are aware of non-verbal communication at every level. When you're fighting with them, or even mentally within yourself, they're going to feel the emotions you are running over and over again in your mind. I practice this in my seminars, to show where a person can emit an energetic emotion to another person they've never even met and you can watch that emotion.

To do this, I have the participants pair up. One participant writes a negative emotion down on a card but doesn't show it to the person they're paired up with. Then, I take the person who hasn't seen the card into a highly relaxed receptive state of light hypnosis. I have the other person focus their energy on the word on the card, be it happiness, love, anger, hate, whatever it is. As they are doing so, the other person in the highly relaxed state now has the ability, even in the environment of the seminar, to pick up on that emotion.

These are the baby steps that start you on the way to becoming a full-fledged runner when it comes to accessing your own mind's power. You can begin to practice what you're able to do on an energetic level. You have the ability as you escalate this and improve to actually know what others are thinking. Is that powerful or what?

The first thing you need to do is become centered. By this I mean find that ability, which you have, to pull yourself from external distraction and into the moment, into the flow. It is also helpful to find somebody to practice these same strategies with you.

With your partner, sit in a comfortable position, facing each other. Once both of you are relaxed, begin to match their breathing. Sitting there, breathing, relaxed, look into each other's eyes. Use your imagination here, remembering that your subconscious cannot differentiate between what is imagined and what is real. Using your imagination, trade places in your mind and become your partner watching you. Basically, enter into a disassociated state where you are your partner watching you.

As you do this, notice the shifts and the minor variables in your energy output and energy feelings. Over time, you'll gain control over more of your energetic exchanges as you send and receive. Send your partner a message, and picture yourself sending them sending you a message. This creates a congruent flow of energy.

Practices like this help you to learn to monitor yourself and take inventory of yourself. This is helpful for when you have an emotionally energetic moment. Say you become angry, for example. When this happens, if you are practicing self-awareness, you are more likely to become aware of the next person you come into contact with, and you will know whether or not you are exhibiting and transferring this energy. We are always receiving, so as you give out love, compassion, and empathy to others, they're drawn to you because these are pleasurable energies, they draw people in rather than repel them.

When you are able to create this energy exchange at will, you can actually begin to read thoughts by feeling other people's thoughts, and science has proven thoughts are energy. However, when it's not understood, you don't look at it as a gift; you begin to look at it as annoyance. Yet this is a gift, even if you're experiencing taking on another person's negative energy, don't see this as "they make me nervous."

Rather, see this as the beginning—you are beginning to develop your own energetic pathways to and from the receiver to the giver, and that is the indication you have the ability to receive. It follows that if you have the ability to receive, you have the ability to give. Consider the ways this skill can change your life, the more you develop it. Imagine all the times you have been nervous or frightened by others' energy. What makes their energy more important or more predominant than yours? Nothing. What an impact you could have on people if instead of taking on that nervous or angry energy you instead could pass to them your calm, grounded energy. That is true power.

Of course, nowhere is the give and take in a relationship more pronounced and vital to understand than in our intimate relationships. Yet before we can even get into the give and take, what is happening between two people when they first come together in these relationships?

In regards to the formation of intimate relationships, there are some general rules that apply. Of course, there are always exceptions to any rule; however, we can operate under a statistical analysis of just how relationships work most effectively. In order to truly create an effective intimate relationship, like with a boyfriend/ girlfriend/ partner/ husband/ wife, your lifestyles need to align to a certain degree. Interests can vary, but the lifestyles need to align.

What do I mean by this? Well, put it this way: If one person is extremely active in the outdoors, and the other person prefers luxury to camping, then what often happens is an overcompensating mechanism develops. This is where one person overcompensates in order to be liked and accepted by the other person. Relationships where this is happening work for a period of time, but many times the other person just really doesn't like that lifestyle, and the lifestyle permeates every part of that person's being. Loving the outdoors, for example, is not a hobby, it's part of a lifestyle. The lifestyle of an extremely active person, in general, is the complete opposite of a sedentary person. So you can see how, if an active and a sedentary person come together, even if they both love the music of Beethoven, the extreme differences in lifestyle can cause conflict within the relationship.

Examine the flipside of this, however, where two active individuals come together with their lifestyles aligned. Within their lifestyles they can still have varying interests— one may play tennis, one may be a runner, one may hate Beethoven, the other may love Beethoven, but the probability of this relationship being a success is far higher, because their lifestyles are aligned. People's interests are just subtle variances, variances that are much easier to accept than total lifestyle mismatch.

This misunderstanding of the difference between lifestyle and interests is the root of why so many people attempt to create massive change in another individual. They get all excited when they start dating or falling in love, because their interests might be aligned, but they neglect to pay attention to the fact that their lifestyles are not aligned at all. So they try to pull the other into their lifestyle, or worse, force them into their lifestyle, or vice versa.

I recall working with a couple when I ran seminars to smaller groups many years ago. In this particular seminar, we were discussing relationships. This couple was made up of an athletic man and a sedentary woman. The man was really active, he was involved in martial arts, he loved swimming, he loved surfing, he enjoyed running, and the woman didn't like any physical activity, at all. When Christmas came, he gave her workout gloves, protein powder, a gym membership, all these things catering to fitness—which was reflective of his lifestyle, not hers—and at the time she pacified the situation and received the gifts gracefully. That was an attempt at moving her into a lifestyle she had no interest in. Meanwhile, he was not interested in sitting around eating junk food and watching sitcoms because he did not enjoy life when lived in that state. If both people liked movies and he liked drama and she liked comedy, their lifestyles would align when they watch movies together because they both would be enjoying the activity. Their interests can still vary, maybe they would choose a comedy one night and perhaps a drama the next. However, it would be much less confrontational for him to watch a movie of her choice, and the same goes for her. The couple in my seminar, however, it was soon to be revealed, had not enough even in terms of interests to overcome the huge mismatch in their lifestyles. Therefore, when the dynamics of a dysfunctional relationship start to appear, it is worth looking to see where they are rooted: Are your lifestyles aligning, or are your interests aligning?

We generally seek out people who share our lifestyles or our interests, or both, if we know to pay attention to the difference, when seeking our life partners. What other criteria do you consider? When it comes to the relationship you have with yourself, what level of criteria are you setting to mandate success in that relationship? I've seen men go on dates, who later shared with me that they felt like they were on an interview, that the date involved their being scrutinized against some sort of checklist formed by the woman around what she thought she wanted in a man and it was clear she would not settle for less.

We want to find someone who meets our needs and who is compatible, but when we move into interacting and communicating and it seems more like an interview where we size each other up, and when we do this, the potential for emotional interaction is rendered null and void.

Love is really an energy. Love is an energy that you feel. You cannot quantify this energy, the energy of love, on a piece of paper, so although it is often recommended that we have criteria when seeking a mate, it is important that the criteria is not so limiting or unforgiving that it leaves no room for things we couldn't have imagined.

I remember another story, this one of a female friend of mine who went on a date once with a great guy. She told me she cared for the guy, after all, he was handsome, successful, funny—everything she wanted in a man. He displayed one small mannerism at the dinner table, something that had to do with eating his food in some form that she didn't agree with, and it was a deal breaker for her. This is an example of criteria that might be too stringent. We have to allow some kind of latitude for human behavior. When you are involved in an intimate relationship with an individual, you'll see behaviors that are part of being human. She is not going to show up wearing a beautiful dress and makeup all the time, and he's not going to be perfectly groomed every time.

Conditioning yourself for a degree of acceptance will actually translate into gratitude for the authentic human being in your life. Gratitude that you have somebody who is there at all, someone to weather the storms with you, to be there when you're not at your best, and accept you when you're not having a good day.

Sometimes we set criteria because we believe we deserve the best. I will certainly not tell you that you don't deserve the best; it is a hallmark of good self-esteem to only expect the best and know that you are deserving of this. But 'the best' is entirely subjective, of course, and I encourage you to determine what your 'the best' is. After all, once true love blossoms and deepens, even the things that really bugged you on the first date about someone have the potential to become endearing. So there is holding out for your view of 'the best,' but holding it loosely will be really what brings the best to you. I've seen people living in near poverty that experience a level of happiness and harmony in relationship much greater than people living in mansions driving around in Mercedes-Benz cars! It has to do with the energy synchronization and the ability to check that compatibility based on open criteria. You can still align with what your baseline is, but you must allow people to be human and not a robotic interpretation of what you feel you deserve.

As I mentioned earlier, love is an energy. When you give love, love comes back to you. So a good rule of thumb is to never love anything that cannot love you back. If you think, "Well, duh, Jim, that goes without saying" let me assure you, it's an important distinction to make. I have known people in my life that really and truly loved their Porsches. I have known people that love their pieces of Tiffany jewelry. I'm suggesting that you like your car, but don't love your car with the full energy of the emotion. You can love your dog, because the dog will give love back, and you can love people, because they have the ability to reciprocate that love too. This creates a flow in the exchange of energy. So you can like your car and your house very much, but to expend actual love into an inanimate object is where you will get in trouble because you're not going to get anything back. Love is an energy that has the ability to not only feed others, but, through reciprocity, feed yourself, and this is powerful because it benefits all parties involved.

Creating healthy relationships and keeping this part of your life in health and alignment is worth every ounce of energy you spend on it. But for some of you, you might find you are not attracting to you the people you desire, or any people. It's not entirely uncommon as we go through life to find our social lives changing over time. Where we once were surrounded by peers and the potential for new peers when we were in public school, high school, and college or university, we may now find ourselves wondering why it is so difficult to make new friends, or find our partners. In a business capacity, if you are an entrepreneur, you might wonder how to attract new clients so you can enter into business relationships. Whether it's love, friendship, or business relationships, you need to cultivate your authentic self, and from the most authentic place you can find, begin to emanate that self around everyone with whom you interact and engage.

This brings me to talking about charisma. Now, you might wonder why I'm including this section on charisma in a book like this. It is because, as I said at the start of this chapter, all life is relationship. Your life is a series of interactions, interactions with yourself, with your peers, with your boss, your teachers, your coaches, your families, your lover, your friends. What you may not realize is that you bring yourself to these interactions and that in each interaction there are two exchanges that take place. One is the exchange between your tangible self and the other individual's tangible self. By this I am referring to your body language, tonality, facial expressions, content delivery, voice, and tone. Beyond this, however, there is also an intangible or energetic exchange. This intangible exchange is more powerful than people understand. When a person has charisma, it means they have the ability to engage powerfully with other people in both tangible and intangible methods of exchange. Now, despite what you may believe charisma to be, let me tell you, there are people that are charismatic living in mansions, as one might assume, and there are also people who are charismatic living in mud huts. There are charismatic people all over the world. Charisma is not the sole party trick of the rich and powerful. The more you understand charisma, the more you can use it yourself to help attract and persuade others in your life. It can help to draw to you the lover you have been seeking, or it can help you to become the leader you know you want to become.

Charisma as it applies to you in creating your own life masterpiece is the ability to bring the best version of yourself to the table. In order to bring the best version of yourself to the table, you need to retain your authenticity of being. This means that you show up as *you*, not as a *form* of you. This generates the energetic response that you'll project to other people, and ultimately if you are able to control it and actually bring it to audiences or groups, and get it into a spatial domain, it really has to be embedded in authenticity; otherwise, internal conflict will result, and that will affect the response of other people.

Charismatic people project confidence, self-worth, and self-assuredness. In other words, they are comfortable in their own skin, whether they are short or tall or whatever, it doesn't matter what they do for work or how they look, they are able to project charisma to other people. What makes somebody receive another as a charismatic person is they see they can fill their own deficits within themselves vicariously through the other person. By this I mean that often we are drawn to leaders and other charismatic and confident people because they can vicariously fill the void that exists in ourselves.

The human body, the human mind, the human spirit, and, indeed, human existence is meant to function harmoniously, holistically, and with fulfillment. You'll have a tendency, when you're very charismatic, to draw people to you who are seeking your strength. Meanwhile, on a deeper level, you're fulfilling the void that exists within them. We have a tendency as humans to be drawn to charismatic people—subordinates are drawn to leaders, for example. People with low self-esteem are drawn to people with high self-esteem. People who are economically uncertain are drawn to people that know how to make an income or invest wisely. What people are drawn to is what they experience in the tangible exchange, so the body language, tonality, delivery of content, but also, and perhaps more importantly, the intangible or energetic response.

As you learn to use your subconscious more effectively, you can use it to learn all of its output mechanisms. One of the most fascinating output mechanisms is the ability to control the energetic response. If you look at Kirlian photography, this energetic aspect of ourselves is called an aura. If you think the concept of aura sounds too 'woo-woo,' let me assure you, science has proven its existence. And you can learn to expand your aura, thereby deepening the impact your energetic response has on those you seek to draw towards you.

I would like to share a technique with you right now that I invite you to put into practice. And be patient with yourself as you begin this work—remember, every virtuoso was once a student!

This technique is about engaging the energetic response. First, read through the next paragraph so you know what the exercise entails.

Take a deep breath and close your eyes. When you close your eyes, try to picture and feel the best version of yourself right now. Use your imagination here, your mind's eye, as it were. From being in this place of the best version of yourself, picture yourself extending your arms, all the way to left and all the way to the right, so your hands are extended directly out on the left and right. Then open your eyes and become aware, using your peripheral vision, of how far you can see. With practice, you should be able to see your fingertips if you wiggle them.

Part of what is happening in this exercise is you are increasing your peripheral vision. But your mind has peripheral vision too, which will also be increased with practice. Close your eyes again and now place a blue light around your head in your mind's eye. Then infuse that light with the authenticity of yourself as an individual. Infuse the light with confidence and self-esteem, and use your imagination as you do this. Move away from literal interpretation of the experience and use your imagination such that you truly see that you are infusing a blue light around your head, that is, an aura, with your authentic self. The subconscious mind will support you to craft whatever you are doing, based on your input. Now extend this blue light, retaining the force and the saturation of what you placed in it—which is the energy of your authentic self—and expand it to where it now goes out approximately four feet to the left and four feet to the right. You are now extending the energetic force of your subconscious mind to create a circumference all the way around you.

Why am I asking you to do this, you may be wondering?

There's an energetic flow you can control that exists about eighteen inches out from your head in your personal space, and you can extend it and push it out even farther until eventually you push it out—while still retaining its density of power—into an entire room.

This speaks to how there are people that can see someone walk into a room, which might cause them to look up, and there are people that feel someone walk into a room—without even looking to see. This is similar to the phenomenon that happens in groups, for example a group of happy people will exude a collective energy that is happy, that you can feel, while a group of people who are emotionally charged will exude that charge, and again, you will feel it.

You control your charismatic energy as you push it out. As you begin to control it from eighteen inches around your head to a wider circumference, over time and with practice you will be able to push it out to about twenty feet in diameter. But don't start with this immediately! Try this exercise the next time you are in a restaurant. Close your eyes, saturate your mind with the most authentic version of yourself, love yourself, and then extend out eighteen inches to a four-foot circumference, and beyond this to twenty feet. Once you start practicing this, and increase that circumference, you will notice people at other tables begin to look over at you—even without you moving or making a noise. It may sound unbelievable, but try it and watch what happens! There are people that have the ability to actually point out a person sitting with their back turned to them, and create such a strong charismatic energy field that they can pick that person out and tell whoever they are with that, "Watch—within ninety seconds that person will turn around!" This is because now they have taken that circular energy field and, using an even more advanced concept that I share only in my seminars, they have condensed that energy field and turned it into a targeted beam and directed that into that person. It sounds strange, but we all know people can sense someone standing behind them or in space. This happens because there is a disruption of their energy field. So in the case of the anecdote I just relayed, the only reason that person is turning around is because their energy field was disrupted and their sensory mechanism has prompted them to turn around. If you try this in a restaurant, select someone who is daydreaming. Anyone who is on their cell phone or engaged in conversation won't be aware. Try it on someone who is in a mentally detached mode while sitting there in order to see it work. Imagine a calm pool of water, when you throw a pebble into it you can see the ripples it makes. But if you throw a pebble into the surf in the ocean, you don't notice the reaction, because the ocean is already so active. So if you try this out, be looking for an inactive mind, to create an active response.

Never underestimate the power of charisma. Once you master this, you now have the building blocks to become a powerful charismatic person. This is a very powerful asset for you to possess as you go through life. It makes life easier in virtually all instances where you need to interact with others. It contributes to people having an innate level of agreement with you, and once they agree—because of that charisma—it makes it easier to guide each of you to the win-win outcome of whatever the situation is.

When you become charismatic, everything becomes easier from a persuasion and influence standpoint. I'm not talking about manipulation; I'm talking about influencing your children, colleagues, or friends. By influence, I mean you are being the director and others are the recipients of your direction. It's not to be used in an ill-fated way. It's to be used positively, because if you're positive that you are crafting the path that is mutually beneficial for someone and yourself, then by all means, clearing the barriers and expediting a smooth journey to that end destination will be in everybody's self-interest.

When you're clearing the barriers, the deeper you get into this work of using your subconscious mind, the more you can even direct each communication interaction you engage in. Communication is truly a way to embed yourself firmly in your destination. We are in a constant state of communication with others. Just as relationship is integral to our lives as humans, communication is a close second in importance. When you are interacting with others, try to drop out of the old story of who's right and who's wrong. Engage in active listening and assimilate the information the other person is saying as the collection of data it is. This data will allow you to assess, analyze, and construct what you want to communicate back to the person with whom you are communicating. All too often, we listen to respond. We don't really listen to the other person, because something they say may spark us and set our brains off generating a response to this person. When you are fixated on what your response will be, you stop listening to what the other person is saying.

Missing the content of the other person's words, however, is like closing the door they are trying to open in this communication. You don't want to miss what's behind the door. Think of it like peeling back the layers of an onion; you are really looking for that core message coming out of the interaction. Core value elicitation is a powerful communication technique that, when paired with active listening, allows you to get to the real message of the interaction. The more you can get to the meat of the message, and the more reserved you are in the exchange, the more you can create the outcome you are hoping for. Because, let's face it, in virtually every interaction where we are communicating with others, there is an ideal outcome we seek from the exchange.

But let's say someone wanted to sell you something. The more you listen, regardless of whether or not you like or agree with what they're saying, the more you will learn. Interacting with people who are better communicators than yourself will teach you a lot about good communication. If you appreciate where they are coming from in the exchange, you will initiate an energetic response that they will sense. Once the person senses that you appreciate where they are coming from, the door is open and you can have a conversation using tactics of persuasion, charisma, and influence that will allow you to guide the conversation in such a way that the outcome you have already anticipated and decided would be ideal will come to fruition.

Understanding charisma and creating that masterful power that everybody seeks, or that persuasive power from the inside, can be helpful when trying to improve your relationships or attract a love relationship. One of the things you want to create is a pulling mechanism, where people are drawn to you. The more they're drawn to you, the less you have to pursue them. I'm talking about holding people's attention—and that's far beyond getting their attention. It's easy to get someone's attention, you just have to clap your hands, shout, speak in a different tone of voice, or put a hand on their shoulder and this will get their attention. Maintaining people's attention, on the other hand, is completely different.

Think of it this way: The longer you listen to a song on the radio, the more engaged in the song you become, and the more the rhythm and melody begins to move you. The longer you are holding someone's attention, the more you are beginning to move them. Using these strategies, you'll learn you can create that charismatic move—but holding people's attention is paramount.

People will never give you their *interest* unless you can keep their attention. People confuse someone glancing at them or nodding their head as interest, but it's not. True persuaders, true people with charisma, will pull the interest from others. What you want is to have people draw in to you as if you were a rubber band, where you are one end, and the person is the other, and you pull the rubber band to full extension—and the end pulls back to you. This is what we talk about when we say the oft-heard phrase, "I was drawn to him/ her." You are trying to tune people in to where they are on your frequency, and then you are able to utilize your personal charisma. Remember that most people that approach you are wearing that social veneer or that shell or mask they go out into society with, so you need to pull them, from a conscious level, back into themselves first, then consciously synchronize in that state with them. It's important that you make people aware of you. One of the strategies you can use is to ask questions and become unique in your response, even in an icebreaker-conversation situation. Discard generic responses because they cause generic reactions.

I'm talking about the kind of generic reactions you have dozens of times a day without thinking about it. Say you're at the coffee shop and the person at the counter asks, "How are you?" This is your chance to discard the generic response. You might choose to say, "Fine," like the other twenty people in line before you, but I would rather encourage you to say something that is not generic, maybe something like "My life is perfect!"

Try it! The next time you interact with somebody, say, "My life is perfect!" Doing this reaffirms your personal charisma and enforces it, but watch the other person's reaction. As you begin to monitor and become aware of others' reactions as you utilize the strategies, it will reinforce your own response. It's like a singer receiving applause, the applause reinforces their validity and talent as a singer.

You have the talent to become a charismatic person; all you have to do is learn techniques like these, and put them into practice. In this example, the non-generic response of

"My life is perfect!" begins to pull the person in. Then you can start to hold their attention.

One way to do that is to ask questions that are completely foreign to the conditioned responses they're used to hearing. Not even crazy questions, per se, but even questions like, "What's your favorite type of music?" when not expected will keep their attention. This kind of activity, where you say the unexpected in a fairly typical scenario, is called a pattern interrupt. This is a hypnotic technique that allows the mind to open the subconscious mind just for a moment. The question about music is not an intrusive question, it's actually a question of interest in an area most people have an answer for. Because it's out of the normal interchange between two people, then when you ask that question you're going to be able to immediately hold their attention because you've stated a question of interest outside of the normal, "What do you do" "Where are you from" and so on. Those are standard responses and keep you standard. I'm inviting you to consider stepping out of the norm when you interact with people

When you ask that individual, "What's your favorite music," they'll be stunned or their response will be, "Hmmm, I wonder why they're asking me that?" One thing is for sure—they will respond. They will respond because you have now displayed a uniqueness, and charismatic people are unique. Charismatic people are not the majority, and they are not part of the masses that walk around in a trance. They know where they're at, they know their purpose, and they display it.

You're going to become one of those people if you practice those techniques. You could say, "Tell me about your favorite pet," and the person you are asking will wonder why you said that. Now is your chance to use the strategies for the holding of attention—mirroring, matching, pacing, and leading. People need to find you interesting, sure, but this will happen by your being interested in them. And the way they find you unique is not by asking generic standard questions.

I have a good friend who likes to tell a story about being on an airplane and sitting next to a woman with whom he struck up a conversation. He barely said ten words the whole time, and after the flight she turned to him and said, "That's the most interesting conversation I've ever had." Understand, you're going to draw people in, then give them the line to go. Draw them in, then release the line to let them fly free. Then you'll have a push-pull charismatic attraction, and they'll say, "I like this person!" This technique is easily used and applicable. You can apply this in your day-to-day life. Start by discarding generic responses. This means no more "I'm fine" when someone asks how you are; rise up to a place that clearly indicates to the person you are interacting with that there's something different about you. Use an interesting response as an initial attention-getter, then, if the conversation continues, ask a question that is not normal. That person now knows you're interested, and you are unique and people like unique! Who do we read books about? Unique people! Who do we watch movies about? Unique people! Who do we talk about? Unique people!

Your charismatic response will create a ripple effect through your closest contacts into their contacts, into strangers, into groups, and ultimately into audiences and into the world. To create a life masterpiece, you have to be a firm believer in yourself. As you move through the book and practice these strategies, your life will be crafted exactly as you want it—it's life by design, not life by circumstance.

Chapter Seventeen: Financial Wealth

Quite possibly trumping the importance of good health and great relationships is the value we have placed on money in current society. Money is not only truly dominating in the collective psyche, it is also an incredibly loaded subject for many. Indeed, the topic of money can fill its own book (and it has, many of them!). For our purposes, let's investigate how to apply the strategies and techniques outlined in earlier chapters to help you program your subconscious mind to accept that the world is abundant. This means pinpointing and working to overcome all limiting beliefs around money that you might have.

The world we live in is a truly abundant world. The universe out of which we were created continues to create and expand, and part of this natural expansion is sheer abundance. This is not a pipedream or another Pollyanna-style belief. This is the truth. Don't believe me? Then tell me how many drops there are in the ocean. Tell me how many grains of sand there are on the beach. If that's too expansive, look closely at a tree sometime and observe how it grows taller, its leaves constantly forming and dying, forming and dying. The tree flowers, bears fruit, sleeps all winter, flowers, bears fruit... you get the picture. If this still isn't enough, consider the trillions of dollars that are actually in existence in the world. It is not for a lack of dollars that there is injustice, suffering, or people who lack. That is about distribution. And we cannot justify lack by looking at how we distribute it. I encourage you to recognize the world as truly abundant and expansive.

I encourage you to start looking for abundance in your daily life. More things happen in your favor each morning before you even step out of bed! Look around your home, in your fridge, look in the basement, at boxes of things you don't need that just sit there. Once you decide to look for evidence of abundance in the world, it is incredibly easy to find. When you fail to see abundance, what you experience is fear of scarcity and a feeling of lack, or 'not enough.' Just because you feel lack or only choose to see what is lacking is not an argument for the lack of abundance in the world. For, echoing everything this book has already been saying, it is how you think that affects your perception. If you choose to hold thoughts of lack, you will only see that which is lacking. This is why I am going to suggest that you start to cultivate thoughts of abundance.

Of course, by now you may have expected I might say that. I say it because it is what I know to be true. When we keep ourselves in a mindset of scarcity or lack, we do not receive the true flow of abundance into our lives. Money, ultimately, is an exchange, an energetic exchange using a modality that has been agreed upon; namely, paper currency. Money needs to be in circulation at all times for any economy to thrive, just like your blood needs to stay circulating in your body for you to stay alive. Money also needs to circulate in order to feed your own economy. When you notice in your life that you are hoarding your money, chances are good that more money is also not flowing towards you. Moving from a mindset of scarcity into the mindset of abundance is one of the single most important steps you can take when deciding to shift your consciousness around money. Seeing that money is an energy that needs to stay in flow and circulate, just like the blood in our bodies needs to circulate, is essential for anyone who is serious about welcoming more money into their lives and understand the need to stay in this flow.

So, adopt an abundance mindset. But let me back up first. Recall from the discussion we had earlier in this book that we have deep-rooted beliefs, beliefs from our parents and their parents and their parents, even, that were planted into our subconscious minds from a very early age. We have been programmed by our life experiences, and through the teachings of influential people in our lives, their experiences too. For any of you who had parents or grandparents who lived through the Great Depression, you in particular may have taken in some strong beliefs of lack and scarcity when it comes to money. You might have heard, "We can't afford (this or that)" every day as a child, or witnessed your parents holding their heads in their hands as they contemplated the bills, worried expressions on their faces. Even people who managed to become wealthy as adults often hoard their wealth because of fears of scarcity they never cleared from their subconscious mind. It's important to note that although you can generate wealth without clearing these beliefs, you won't necessarily keep it. Or you will only generate as much as you believe you can have. Generally, people who are wealthy and hoard their wealth are operating from a fear of lack and scarcity mindset. You may think the family with 'old money' are wealthy, but if they have hoarded all their 'old money' you can guarantee no new flow of money has been coming to them. Despite what you may perceive, millionaires don't always remain millionaires for life. Things are never what they seem. Putting some effort into clearing your limiting beliefs around money is essential and it is best done prior to setting to work adopting the abundance mindset.

Keep in mind, as well, that just having money is not always the solution to the problem. It is important to truly assess whether or not you want money itself, or the feeling of being secure. The two are not necessarily the same. Millionaires can feel stress around money and the constant need to have more just as much as someone who is living on food stamps. The action is to get rid of your limiting beliefs around money first and foremost, and then to establish clear money goals for your life, keeping in mind goals that serve your ability to use money for good, not just to buy yachts or be excessive.

Common limiting beliefs around money include, "I don't deserve to be rich," or "no one in our family is rich," or "money doesn't grow on trees." There are also beliefs around how to get money, with one of the deepest entrenched beliefs being that of go to college or university to learn a skill, go to work for someone else, buy a house, put money into a 401K, retire. For many, they simply do not believe that wealth can come to them any other way. While sure, it may be the most common way, by no means is this the only way to earn a sound income.

In fact, this is an incredibly limiting way to look at how you might earn money in the world. When you look at the idea of making money solely within this paradigm, you are looking at living the life of a worker only. There is no inherent room for growth or leadership in this paradigm (although it does cultivate managers and CEOs). It is a tight fit for anyone who is creative and entrepreneurial. I know for myself, I knew as a young man that was not the route I wanted to take. My father and brother, both university-educated and successful, thought I was foolish, but now I have surpassed both of them in annual income, by being an entrepreneur. If I had stayed in the belief that I could only make money following that formula, I certainly would not be where I am now, having already sold two successful companies (both for seven figures), and running three even more successful companies today.

To clear limiting beliefs, you can access your subconscious mind in the way I outlined in chapter eleven. While you are doing this, at the same time you can begin to emotionalize your belief that you are wealthy by picking the number of dollars you really want. By this, I mean the amount of money that would truly make you comfortable right now in your life, and really visualizing that amount. You might come to this number by taking an honest look at your financial situation, and adding to it what realistically will help to make you live comfortably. Don't necessarily reach for the blanket "one million dollars" right away. Be thoughtful. Be practical. Once you have the number in mind, write it down. Visualize it. Add the emotion of what you will feel when you have that amount, and really try to stay in that emotion, especially when paying your bills or doing anything related to your finances at any time of day.

You don't necessarily have to clear your limiting beliefs to start adopting an abundance mindset, although it helps greatly to at least know what your limiting beliefs are. Moving out of a mindset of lack and into one where you truly know and feel the abundance that is all around you won't happen overnight. In fact, it might be worth teaming up with others who want to shift into this mindset, especially at the beginning, because the scarcity paradigm is so incredibly insidious. It is common and everywhere. Think about your friends and family—can you think of a person who truly lives in abundance daily? Be clear—living in an abundance mindset doesn't mean the person is super-rich, necessarily. But a person living in an abundance mindset comes from a place of knowing their needs are met. This person knows that they have the skill, talent, and resilience required to achieve their money goals. This person also is fully aware that they have Universal Power backing them up when they take action. And take note of that word, action, for action is essential here. You will receive support only if you take concrete action in your physical reality that will get you closer to your financial goals. Taking action in the physical world is essential. However, visualizing clearly the amount of money you want with a strong emotionalization component plus taking action, alongside a healthy dose of abundance mindset, will definitely form a strong team to help you on your journey to financial abundance.

A person in abundance mindset is acutely aware that there is more than enough of everything in the world—

water, food, land, space, air, money. A person in abundance mindset is not afraid of the competition, but rather welcomes the competition and knows there is plenty for all. A person in abundance mindset is not afraid to give and gives freely, knowing full well that the more they give, the more they receive. (As an aside, this statement, really an old adage, is entirely true. For anyone who doubts me on this, I highly recommend you embark on giving one thing daily for twenty-one days, and pay close attention to what you receive. I assure you, this experiment will blow your scarcity mindset out of the water, and fast!)

To be in abundance mindset is to be in faith. To be in faith means that you know, really know, throughout every plane of existence and right to your very core, that you have access to the Universal Power that your subconscious mind connects you to. You also have full knowledge and understanding of the Law of Attraction, the most commonly talked about concept when it comes to shifting money consciousness. When you move beyond just using the Law of Attraction and use the techniques you have just read about in previous chapters, then you are truly employing powerful means to help you generate the wealth you desire. Of course, remember, the Law of Attraction and even my techniques don't necessarily bring you the money—poof!— by dropping a bag of cash on your doorstep the next morning. However, your working of these tools and using the Law of Attraction allows you to be open to receiving the circumstances that pave the way for manifestation. Ideas will come along, a job will present, the right person will cross your path, that investor you were looking for, etc. Shifting your money consciousness just grants all of these opportunities a clearer path of access to you.

There are two other essentials, however, to generating wealth. Along with clearing limiting beliefs and adopting an abundance mindset, it is important to consider your work as how you serve others, and to always maintain a feeling of gratitude.

Your work is your service to the world. If you don't like your work, you may want to investigate what it is that you do like, what your skills and talents are, and how you can help people. When we reframe our 'work' to become about how we can help others, we are able to derive more meaning from what we do. It is definitely true, as I have witnessed, that the more we serve others, the more money shows up in our lives. The money shows up in proportion to the service we provide. So if you are not earning a lot of money, it's possible you are not serving enough people. If money is a tool we use as an exchange for value given, then it follows that you must give service, and service with value, to another in order to generate the income you desire. Financial wealth is created through using your work to provide a valuable service to others, and the more people you serve and bring value to, the wealthier you will become. Why do you think someone like Bill Gates is so wealthy? How much value did he bring into your life just by creating Microsoft? How much value did he bring to millions of people, for that matter? This correlates directly with the billions he has amassed in money thanks to his ingenuity. Bill Gates saw a problem that needed to be solved, and he solved it for millions of people. This is why it is faster, often, to increase your wealth by being in sales or being an entrepreneur, as both afford more opportunities to be providing your unique service and value to people, versus jobs like being a doctor. Being a doctor is a hugely important role in the fabric of society, don't get me wrong, but there is a limit on just how many patients a doctor can see in a day and therefore a limit to their service, and a limit to the wealth they can accumulate in an authentic way.

This may seem like a limiting conversation and it's possible that for some of you reading this that you just do not see the value inherent in your jobs. However, be aware, every job is a service to humanity. When it comes to creating more wealth in your life, even if you are working a minimum-wage job as you read this, it is entirely possible for you to achieve the wealth you want if you get out of your limiting beliefs, adopt an abundance mindset, and see the value in who you are and what you do. We should not be chasing money for money's sake, remember. Finding your way to true wealth will look different for every individual. Finding your way to *sustaining* true wealth involves doing the work in this book.

Be of service, and cultivate a feeling of gratitude. Gratitude goes hand-in-hand with living in an abundance mindset. You don't have to wait to be grateful. Start feeling grateful today, right now. Be grateful for absolutely everything you have in your life, everything, and tune into your gratitude at least once daily. An incredibly common practice around gratitude that everyone from Oprah to any random life coach on the internet has suggested is the practice of keeping a gratitude journal. Well, why do you think they suggest it? Because it works! It doesn't have to be a gratitude journal, per se, that you keep, but cultivating and maintaining a feeling of gratitude, coupled with unwavering belief in the abundance of the universe, truly does serve to keep you in the flow of wealth accumulation.

Remember throughout all of this that your subconscious mind responds to your conscious thoughts, particularly repeating thoughts, and does not distinguish the negative thoughts from the positive ones. Therefore, if you are rattling around in your mind a constant barrage of poverty-talk, you must reframe those thoughts. Ideally, you will clear these beliefs at the level of the subconscious mind, but even if you don't or if it takes time, you can and must choose to hold thoughts that support your vision of wealth. Hold thoughts that support your being rich. Recall the exercises I mentioned in chapter eleven, and really see the Mercedes-Benz when you think of it. Daydreaming is allowed! The subconscious mind responds to visual and emotional stimuli. See it, know you have it, believe you have it, and think you have it. Amplify the Law of Attraction by using the rules of the mind. Build on all of this by truly living from a place of abundance, and you will achieve all that you desire.

If choosing to hold thoughts of abundance still feels like too much work to start, then at the very least get a handle on the repeating story you have running about money, and reframe those thoughts. I'm sure you must have friends whose mantra is "I can't afford it!" If you are one of those people, you might start shifting by reframing "I can't afford it" to "I am choosing to not spend my money on this at this time." It's all about getting yourself back into the driver's seat, so all those limiting beliefs stop informing every choice you make or how you feel whenever you spend money.

Just like with health and relationships, you can take control of your finances and generate wealth instead of constantly succumbing to circumstance and feeling victim to a system that is inarguably tilted in favor of the wealthy. Just like I said in chapter eight, you *are* the "Other people." The sooner you believe that you can change, that you have Universal Power within you to help generate change, that you can truly create your life the way you want it to be, the sooner you will be living in your own life masterpiece.

By using the techniques outlined in previous chapters, you can pinpoint and eradicate your limiting beliefs. You can use awareness and focus to choose to hold positive, abundant thoughts in place of any thought that comes from a place of lack or scarcity. You can reframe how you see yourself in the world to become more about what you can give, and how you can serve others, as opposed to solely coming from "What's in it for me?" Making time to feel grateful for everything you have in your life—money, love, your dog, your health, the sunset, getting that parking spot so you weren't late for your meeting, anything and everything you are grateful for—assures more goodness to come your way. The world is abundant; whether or not you choose to live in and play in its abundance is entirely up to you. When you do decide to step into what is truly available for you, you can be sure that the Universal Power accessed through your subconscious mind will help you to make your desires a reality.

Part 5: Advancing the Mind

Chapter Eighteen: Exploring New Territory

Hopefully by now, if you have read this far, your curiosity has been sparked and stimulated as to just how far mind can go as an internal entity within yourself and also as a grouped entity, or systematically connected entity, to other energy that is out there. (In particular, the energy of other people.) It's a powerful unexplored territory for most people.

The mind and the body are both systemic and when we look at this, we see there are systems that are working in concert with each other. Whether it be a physical system, like your nervous and respiratory systems, or your mind working systemically to create an internal reality that synchronizes with the external, these systems function without your conscious direction. As the evolution of mind becomes even more apparent to people in the foreseeable future, you will see a profound understanding of all these relationships that have been there, like a computer program running in the background of our lives, for the entire time.

Some of the people that are more developed mentally, psychically, and subconsciously have the ability to pick up on this. We've seen the intuitives in our world do this. There is quite some talent out there when it comes to people who have progressed the innate capabilities of mind, either by circumstances or genetics. Yet, not unlike an athletic body, so too the human mind can be developed. You may not be the most flexible person in the world, but you can consistently stretch until you achieve a high level of flexibility. You might not be the most muscular person, yet with applied effort you can certainly create a muscular physique.

We're often confronted with the objective of realizing the power of the mind without any form of preparation. That is why it is my hope that through this book you gain a fundamental understanding of the processes, and use the techniques at the beginner stage, intermediate stage, and advanced stage. What we are doing here is unlocking the mysteries that will collapse your preexisting beliefs.

Once you delve into your own mind and its capabilities, any preexisting beliefs are dwarfed by this newfound territory. The uncluttered mind is a perfect channel through which conscious awareness of the reality of all of the systemic possibilities that exist can pass—both within your mind as well as with other minds and other energy. Those conscious thought processes that clutter our minds on a daily basis are simply veils that hide our current understanding.

Once we begin to understand this, we end up being able to create a flow of conscious awareness. For you to develop the full potential of your mind, you must include elements that allow you an advantage over the beginning aspects that go beyond just a functional mind.

When I say "functional mind," I am referring to the mind that ninety-nine percent of the population engages in. The functional mind is your conscious awareness that makes conscious choices, while the subconscious is directing behavior based on the emotional platform. We roll through life as though the mind is no different than our hand; like our hand mechanically takes hold of things, the mind grasps things when we want it to, but we otherwise don't engage in the control or self-control of the mind, much less programming the subconscious mind. Using strategies like the ones in this book, along with other techniques like mind-mapping, neuro-linguistic programming, and psychosomatic parenthetics are what will allow you to go from being a beginner, to an intermediate, and finally an advanced student, to where you will really master your most powerful tool.

The mind in everybody's personalized form is actually a feedback mechanism. This means that in order for you to think, you have to be in a certain state of mind, so you're feeding back to yourself. When you're looking at the strategies in this book, like I just mentioned, you're able to disengage from the feedback loop and objectively observe the energetic qualities of mind. Once you're able to do that, you can direct it.

Imagine if you are on a sailboat and sailing, but you are incapable of seeing where the sails are set. If you are a hundred feet in the air, you can see the relationship between the sails, the wind, and the direction in which the boat is going. From that vantage point, you can forecast, and intentionally direct your boat to your desired destination.

It is exactly the same with your mind. Once you understand objectively its capabilities, you can direct it.

However, your mind must be open. It has been said, after all, that "a closed mind is like a closed parachute," and thus an open mind opens possibilities far beyond just the conscious thought. What I'm talking about here is different than having an open mind to a type of music or a lifestyle. An open mind in this context is an open mind that does not self-restrict. Once you have the ability to move forward in an unrestricted fashion, you have the ability to absorb energetic footprints that are not only from yourself, but other people as well.

That is the power of creation that you hold within yourself—the mind in its magnetic form. By this I mean when the mind of a civilization is put in congruence or harmony, we see things happen. For example, if you were to go to a group of people in emotionalized states, say in a church, or at a concert, or at a motivational seminar, you begin to sense the collective energy in the room. There have been studies done where a person has been put in a complete sensory deprivation mode, so they cannot hear or see, and they still sense that there is an energetic grouping in that room. How can this be? They can't see the crowd or the parishioners or hear the music, and they don't feel anything on the physical level, but they feel something energetically.

Now you have the substance that allows you to become aware, and once you become aware you become enlightened, and you have gained personal ground toward progression. The reason this chapter will move into these processes is to not leave you in the intermediate state but to give you the cause and effect of curiosity, anticipatory response, and excitation, because, after all, the mind is an emotional vehicle.

This book is meant to be that catalyst to allow you to understand the fundamentals of the potential that you have. Our excitement comes from the end destination, not the trip. It's the actual destination that excites us. Once the excitement overrides all logistics and things you have to put in place to get there, then your mind moves in the future-pacing strategy. You become more aware of the energetic footprint and how that interacts with other people's minds and groupings together. This energy translates as awareness or flow in your life.

It's like noticing the breeze. Oftentimes I will be out with someone and if there's a light breeze, chances are that the person I am with will not notice it. This is because their mind is not focused on it until I draw their attention to it. Once I point it out to them, then they do notice it. Until that time, they have been functioning in such an automatic way that they have not selectively cued in on the breeze, the birds chirping, or whatever other subtle things may be surrounding them.

Once you have selectively cued in on energy, you can see how energy healing works, how body mind synchronization strategies work, and how my advanced hypnosis strategies work, because we're now becoming selectively aware of each individual component where the outcome is the sum of all the parts.

As you advance the mind, you have to become aware of where the mind originated or at least where it originated in our current form.

No one knows for sure what the mind actually is. The human body can be created, for the most part, in a laboratory with an accumulation of certain substances, yet it would be impossible for them to recreate the mind. They may even come close to recreating the brain, but certainly not the mind. The mind is that ever-elusive component that is unexplainable. Yet, in order for people to understand how to advance the mind, it only makes sense to understand where it came from, or at least our perceived origin.

In the first few moments following birth, we instinctively learned that our life support depended upon other people. Along with this instinctive learning, you also realized that your survival is based on pleasing people in that environment.

This is why to meet with someone's disapproval is actually a very life-threatening experience to people. When you are advancing your own mind, the trick then becomes to synchronize your own self-worth with advancement. As small children, we learned to use inference to get our needs met. For example, we learned that a smile brings acceptance, a scowl or bad behavior brings pain, a hug and being kind brings pleasure, and, as babies, other ways we could get attention as expressed through crying. As we grew older, getting approval and acceptance became of paramount importance, and we learned that we could influence other people through our speech.

When you advance the human mind, it is important to understand the simplicity of the origin and the complexity of the evolution. It is an evolution that is self-contained based on your environmental exposure. So we begin to question what is being said when somebody says it and what are we saying to ourselves when we say it to ourselves. In order to advance the mind, you're going to advance into a world of imagination, so your communication strategies can also be imagined. This becomes very internally stimulating to the subconscious mind, as it accepts everything either as a truism or as real. Recall, the subconscious mind is incapable of differentiating between what is imagined and what is real, so if you are imagining an expansive mind, then the subconscious mind will expand accordingly. It's almost like the inherent push out of a balloon. Most of the time, a balloon will inflate from the outside in, or some influx of air or gas is forced into the balloon. You can produce this same expansion of your subconscious mind through self-inflating, and you do this through use of the imagination. By understanding the origin, you have less pushback or conflict internally.

A mind that is in conflict looks for escape, and a mind that is in harmony looks for growth. If you are able to create an environment which is conducive toward expanding the mind from the subconscious out to the conscious mind, then you can advance the mind into new territories.

Think of the karate student that is able to stretch, as some moves require flexibility as a prerequisite for the move itself. In a similar way, some of the mind's more advanced capabilities require expanding or stretching the mind as a prerequisite to attain that level of mind power. In order to do this, you have the expectation, the anticipation, and the inner expansion occurring by imagining that your mind is expanding. This will have an unconscious affect that will ultimately parlay into a conscious effect on your mind.

Advanced techniques such as parenthetics and psychosomatic parenthetics are things that have been written to create the circular reasoning that people use inside themselves when progressing their minds.

As you do this work, you will move from the beginner level through the intermediate level and into the advanced level before finally entering the imaginative stage. This work is fascinating because nothing has been conquered yet—certainly not the human mind.

Think for a moment now. If you are always seeking solutions, and you can never find the answers, then you aren't using ninety percent of your mind's capacity. But how incredible is your mind? Especially when you realize each connection tries to duplicate in technology what one human brain cell, the neuron, can do. The human brain has over ten to fifteen billion connections and neurons, so it would take literally gigantic advancements in technology to even come close to what our capabilities truly are.

The exploration of this new territory of the mind is not unlike exploring the ocean. Even as I write this, humans have yet to find every crevice of the ocean; it remains under exploration and may stay this way for another several decades. Yet don't we live on a planet where we can go to other planets? And how ridiculous is it that we even pursue interplanetary exploration, given we have not thoroughly explored our own?

The same is true with the human mind. We can explore subjects and develop expertise in subjects outside of our own mind, and yet we leave this vast landscape unexplored. When you look around at all the people who suffer unnecessarily in the world today, for many of them, especially those in North America, it is because they haven't explored the territory that allows the solutions to be accessed.

Your mind is a vast resource and it stores millions of items of information that have been acquired over the years, integrating them and chronologically organizing them for recall. As you have now seen through reading the previous chapters, the mind can be rewired, duplicated, and future-paced. It is a vast arsenal of human power that you actually possess, just sitting inside your own head.

How can you master the complexity of the mind and put it to work for you? It's a marvelous tool. Although I have spent the time outlining its many facets in previous chapters, in truth, you really don't have to be overly concerned with how it works. Just like when I get in my car and press on the gas pedal and the car goes forward—I don't need to know what is going on under the hood to make the car go. In fact, the analytical mind slows down the process of the subconscious mind. We need to just allow our subconscious mind to do its perfect work—and this is what the potential of this book offers to you.

Imagine being able to create a mind so powerful that your life will be the reflection of this newfound power. It is yours, if you apply the strategies we've gone over in this book.

The mind is also a new way of tapping your energy sources. When you explore new territory, you do so by repetition. As the mountain climber climbs a new and higher peak, there may be changes in direction and it may be all new territory. However, the climber has mastered the fundamental techniques of climbing. The fundamentals remain the same, regardless of the mountain he is on, thereby the climber can climb any mountain. The same goes with your mind and advancing your mind into new territory. Once you have the fundamentals, like those covered in earlier chapters, you will be able to master more advanced and imaginative techniques.

After working in the human potential industry for so many decades now, I have seen over and over again people want to skip over the basics. But look at mountain climbers, look at athletes, look at musicians, they all master the basics of their craft. You must master the basics of your mind through practicing the techniques, and the constant insertion of that topic of interest in your conscious thought processes.

Your internal environment will continue to try and program you, so you want to make sure your exploration of this new territory becomes emotionalized. By setting aside the time to study your own mind, you are in the now, and in the flow. And as you remain in that space, you have a very fertile ground for expansive thought.

All too often, people go to meditation classes, read personal development books, take expensive seminars, or attend my self-hypnosis neuro-linguistic programming trainings and they become instantly enamored with the power of the human mind. Yet it always makes me sad because I know the majority will not take time to master this new exploration into this fascinating, profound and endless territory.

It's the same as being fascinated when you first learn scuba diving, only to then leave that untapped resource of the entire vast holdings of the ocean unexplored.

Another thing you'll see as you manifest your own mental acuity and the power of your own mind is a greater awareness of others. Just like we discussed in part four, you'll become somebody that has that ability to attract people, someone who has charisma. I'm not talking about using the Law of Attraction, rather I'm speaking about the ability to attract people because you're different from them. Like doesn't exclusively attract like, even though it has a tendency to do so in rapport building, but setting yourself apart will always remove you from the masses and allow them to know there's something special about you. That something special is the time that you've spent in growing your mind. This will certainly give you a unique positioning in a sea of humanity where very few others, at least in our culture, ever spend any time doing this.

As you venture bravely into exploring this new territory, your confidence and ability will grow. You will see that you have an untapped resource and this new territory will become the very depths of your own inner ocean you can explore for the rest of your life.

Chapter Nineteen: Intuition

When we are accessing this vast and seemingly limitless new territory within ourselves, we have to understand that we are exploring areas within ourselves we have not yet explored. It is imperative that we don't use the normal assumptions, strategies, or metrics we would ordinarily use when analyzing what our internal self is truly capable of. One of the most underexplored elements of our mind and what's available to us as humans is the concept of intuition.

Intuition is the human mind interacting with outside variables and outside influences, an energetic response, not only to yourself, but to outside energy as well.

How does intuition operate? It is easier to explain it by saying what it does *not* do. Intuition is not when the mind figures everything out. Human beings have a tendency to be linear, literal, very organized, and analytical, but intuition does not work like a computer going "1 +2 = 3." It does not use utilize the principles of logic like a computer, nor does it operate in a world of form or structure. And most certainly, intuition is not your ego.

Intuition is the ability to know without words and to sense an inherent truth without any explanation attached. The analytical mind must detach to allow intuition to fully take hold. Intuition doesn't speak to you through certain verifiable insights that you have through past experiences. Rather, it is a feeling that comes up in the form of internally generated words or images or thoughts. As such, intuition will synthesize an idea in a fast moment.

People who really live their lives based on their intuition have a highly honed mind that embraces their ability to be intuitive. You might look at Einstein as an example of just one of the great minds that learned to refine and utilize their intuition.

You can have moments of intuition, and I'm sure we all do, but you can also refine this as your inner territory. As such, it is a place where you can go, a sanctuary of answers, as it were, where all the answers are of purity and not analytically polluted. If you find you are feeling something that is pulling you in a certain direction at any time, that would be your intuition.

Once you begin to realize and understand that intuition is a path you can use to journey on, not unlike so much of the work in developing the mind, you can then think of it as a beam of light. There is no way to step on that beam; there is no way to grab it, compartmentalize it, or take it with you. Yet you cannot deny that it does exist, just as your intuition does. You can certainly interrupt your intuition, however, and we do so by interrupting with analytical, conscious thought. However, if you allow it to happen, the beam of light that is your intuition over time becomes more pure. It purifies to the point where if it were a flashlight, you could take your intuition and condense it down to a laser beam.

So many of the doorways, pathways, outcomes, and circumstances you desire are spawned from and perpetuated by your own intuition. You can find answers to challenges or you can find directional answers not influenced by outside people or influences. Oftentimes, you will be brought to your outcomes much faster if you act on your intuition.

Of course, does that mean your intuition is infallible? Absolutely not, however nothing in this life is a guarantee. All you have is a collection of tools in your toolbox called your mind that you are learning to use.

Does it mean that every time you strike a nail with a hammer the nail will never bend? Perhaps, but now you are taking action toward building something. Does it mean that every time you drive your car it will stay on course? Of course not. But your intuition leads you in the initial direction, a direction that is now garnering information from both Universal Power and your intuitive sense that is synchronizing with it.

Of course, keep in mind as well that one cannot live in the world of intuition alone. People that do this are just fantasizing their lives away. They spend their days lost in daydreams and reverie, wishing about things. Intuition in its best form is the precursor of action. And as we talked about in chapter seventeen, action is what creates the outcome.

When you want to initiate more of your capabilities in the area of intuition, the first step to take is to develop strong self-love. In the simplest of terms, self-love is the ability for you to accept yourself as you are, fully and completely. Accepting both the light and the dark sides of yourself, without regret, guilt, or judgment. How is it that so many people cannot make their own decisions, and look outside themselves when they have one of the most powerful decision-making concepts and decision-making protocols and capabilities within their intuitive mind? It has to do with their lack of accepting themselves and trusting themselves as capable entities—working in tandem with Universal Power—when it comes to directing their own lives. The good news is, intuition can be developed in a person, just like a person can develop athletic capabilities, or become a dancer, or develop musical abilities.

An exercise to start with as you develop your intuition is to write down a series of five questions. These can be questions about anything. Questions like, "What is the best dog for me to get? What is the best city for me to live in? What is my best path in life?" and the like. Questions about anything, really, that you seek a deeper, inner guidance on finding the solution for. Take some time once you have your questions written down, and quiet the mind. Using any technique you like, sit down for a few moments, quiet the mind, and then ask the question. Repeat the question a few times to yourself.

As you listen for the answers, detach and allow. Do not direct, do not hinder, and do not help your mind. Allow your mind to do its perfect work, and then pick up the intuitive thought. As you pick up the thought, also notice how it's delivered.

Another good time to practice this exercise is at night as you go to sleep. At night, your conscious mind goes to sleep and the subconscious mind continues to function. You are in a high state of allowing when you sleep, as you are not interrupting your mind's perfect work with egotistical thoughts, worries, beliefs, and all of the other 'programs' that run when you are awake and perceivably 'in control'. This is a good time to ask your questions, go to sleep, and see what answers present in the first few moments of waking (if they haven't presented in your dreams, that is). Really, any time you can allow your mind to do its perfect work, you will be growing in your ability to access your intuition.

For some people, the answers to the questions you ask of your intuition are delivered in the form of voice in their head, while in others, they receive the answers in the form of a feeling in the body. Everybody is different, so the how your intuition presents to you depends on your unique makeup. You must become further attuned to how your intuition is delivered, however, so when the package arrives, you can open it.

Each and every one of you has this power within you to develop, and as you begin to understand intuition, and become intimately familiar with it, you will be able to utilize it in all areas of your life. You can begin to practice using your intuitive mind in a multitude of ways.

When it comes to practicing and developing your intuition, it is good to think of a challenge that you have in life that may have multiple choices, all leading to different outcomes. For instance, whether or not you should move forward with a new relationship, take a new job, or move. Whatever it is in your life that features the element of choice is what you want to use to create your practice of sharpening your intuitive skills around.

One of the most fascinating ways to work with intuition is to experience a floatation tank. These are essentially sensory deprivation tanks, and they are becoming more and more popular. You can find one in most major cities in North America nowadays. I like to float at least once a week to tap into the deeper levels of my mind. These tanks are really just large tanks of water that has been warmed up to body temperature and filled with Epsom salts, then made to exclude all light and sound. There is no stimuli whatsoever, even your body is not touching anything, when you are in a floatation tank.

It takes about forty minutes for the human mind to shut off from the constant response mechanisms that are initiated internally and to really allow the mind to go into a state of hibernation. Floatation tanks are very restorative, as they allow the body and mind to restore themselves with the exclusion of all external stimuli. As such, floating in these tanks is also an excellent way to learn to tap into the deeper levels of your intuition.

You don't necessarily need to go to a floatation tank to begin to develop your intuition, however. Here is an exercise that you can do as you go to bed at night. Keep in mind, as you do this, to ensure there will be as little external stimuli as possible, and ideally no external stimuli. By this I mean make sure the dog is put away, the kids are fast asleep, the TV, iPod, radio, you name it are all turned off. The room is dark, perhaps your eyes are covered with an eye pad—you get the idea.

It is also a good idea to read through the next section and record yourself reading it on a recording device, so that you can just listen to it when you go to practice it.

Begin by relaxing your feet and ankles. Focus your awareness on your feet and ankles, and really tune in your awareness there. With your awareness on your feet and ankles, allow your muscles to relax like loose rubber bands. Allow them to relax, put your awareness in your feet then move it to your ankles, allow them to relax, then move your awareness to your calves. Allow your calves to relax. Move your awareness to your thighs. Allow your thighs to relax. Move your awareness to your hips. Allow your hips to relax. From feet to hips, your lower part of your body feels like loose rubber bands.

Completely move your awareness to your lower body, as if your body has been cut in half. Allow your entire lower body as a unit to relax. Feel your lower body like loose rubber bands relaxing. Every muscle and nerve relaxing, all the tension flowing out of your body.

Move this relaxation into your abdomen, then into your stomach area. Move the relaxation up through your chest, then down both shoulders and into your biceps and triceps. Move the relaxation down into your forearms, down into your wrists, and all the way to your fingertips. Move from the lower neck, through the neck, into all of your facial muscles and the back of your neck.

Move this relaxation up into the sides of your head, all the way up to the top of your head. Picture your entire body encompassed in relaxation.

In this relaxed state, allow the intuitive mind to open up.

Imagine a ball, about the size of a baseball, made of blue, glowing light, approximately ten feet above your forehead if you are lying down, hovering vertically straight above.

See the word 'intuition' on that glowing blue ball of light. Take a moment and push all of your awareness into that ball. Allow it to resonate in that ball. Allow the ball to gather energy. Sense the energy the ball has, and the energy coming into that ball from all around it, from the environment surrounding it, from the universe.

State out loud the challenge that you have. You might ask something like, "Should I move forward with this relationship?" or "Should I accept that job?" or "Should I move to this new city?" Whatever it is, state it in the form of a question. Then, detach.

Take that glowing ball of light with word 'intuition' and pull it towards you. See it slowly coming towards your forehead, closer and closer, until it touches your forehead, and moves through your forehead and into your mind. Picture this happening. Your mind is doing its perfect work.

Use your sensory awareness and imagination to see the glowing light and intuitive energy permeating every brain cell, everywhere in your mind. Then ask the question once more, and detach.

Stay relaxed and detached from all external stimuli and internal thought processes as best you can. This will take practice, but you'll get it.

Allow, do not hinder or help, but allow the thoughts to flow through your head. You'll have different thoughts on different things, and as you become more in tune, the other thoughts will to go into abeyance and you'll be focused on the answer.

Keep in mind, however, that the answer may not be the answer that you consciously want. But it will be your intuitive answer, based on resonance of universal energy and other components that are far beyond just your conscious mind. Allow the answer to come as it comes. It may come in thirty seconds, fifteen minutes, or in another session altogether.

You can do this practice once a day, or twice a day, and as you see any repetition of intuition, you will know you've found the right answer. Allow it to come, and even if it may not be the answer you are looking for, it will be the answer your intuitive mind has given to you. At that point, you will reach a crossroads of decision. It's very difficult for the analytical mind to grab hold of the intuitive mind, because intuition is not tangible. It's a thought, it's a hunch, it's guidance.

Look at what your inhibition might be about taking that guidance. It could be fear of making the wrong choice. Yet once you begin to follow your intuition, you'll begin to see a pattern of making the best choices that serve you, and you will want to use your intuition as it becomes more in tune with the directions you are seeking in life, and the directions you are seeking become more in tune with utilizing that intuition as your GPS.

Remember, you are developing your intuition. Just as a student of karate will practice moves both for the benefit of the exercise and also to possibly use them for self-defense someday, so too when you practice developing your intuition you are doing so for its own benefit, and so that you may use it as a foolproof guidance tool someday.

That day might be when you do embark on a new love relationship with another. One of the most fascinating uses for your intuition is when you are exploring the polarity of love. When most people think of love, they think of it in the context of being loved, and seldom as the act of loving itself. In other words, they think of what they get, not what they give. As a consequence, their idea of love is unreal, one-sided, and impossible to attain based on these arbitrary parameters they have set. But once you understand that your intuition is what allows for the reciprocal flow of love, then you can really see that it's a give and take, a back and forth, and it's not directed in one way or another.

Most people in modern society set a great expectation on themselves to be the winner. We have a sense of entitlement, we want to be the best entertainer, we want the attention. When you use your intuition, you are now able to bypass the insatiable ego. The ego demands acquisition and attention. Your intuition will show you how to maneuver around the ego toward the purity of love—and love is the only force in the world that is omnipotent. Everything else is a conditional aspect of love; either you experience an absence of it or you have love—it's one or the other.

Remember earlier how I mentioned that love is an energy; well, it is an energy that can be obtained with intuitive understanding. You are able to create an environment within yourself of loving yourself, which also encompasses loving other people. In truth, the desire for love, the very necessity to love, springs from the individual's sense of separateness and isolation. Yet we must love ourselves to truly engage in the real giving and receiving of love as an energy. Many times, your subconscious memories of being in your whole and complete state leaves you recognizing where you are living in an incomplete state, yet your intuitive ability to achieve that complete state of being is there one hundred percent of the time.

The disconnection that is inherent in the human condition, that feeling of separateness and isolation, is one of disconnection from Universal Power. As intuition and the subconscious mind are our direct taproots to this connection with Universal Power, it only follows that when you truly begin to tap into your intuition, it will fill the void cause by this disconnection, separation, and isolation we perceive. When you understand the power of your intuition, it will inherently fill the void you are seeking to fill. Throughout our lives, we use our physical senses to try and fill the void as we experience it. In the worst cases, we stimulate our physical senses using drugs, alcohol, or other modalities that do not serve our best interest. We numb ourselves because the quest for love has become a daunting one. Indeed, the roots of addiction and addictive behavior lie in this disconnection and isolation. However, it is a difficult concept for the non-spiritual minded individual, or people living in total ignorance of the true power of their mind, to truly grasp that we already are that which we seek.

When you use your intuition, it will direct you toward the circumstances, people places, and things that can fill that void. A critical step to remember, however, is they may not always be where your physical senses dictate you go. Oftentimes, we see people in relationships seeking love in the same repetitive environments that are not serving them, and even abusing them physically and emotionally. This is because they're seeking love based solely on their physical needs, or the perceived needs of the insatiable ego. Once love is approached on the intuitive level, love may become reciprocal and flow. Even from a person you never thought you'd be in love with, you can experience the true meaning and purity of emotion of love the more you tap into your intuitive ability

So as you begin this work of tapping into your intuition, focus on the energy of love, and let it embrace everything and allow you to see, with clarity, what void and emptiness you really are yearning to fill.

Consider, if I were to take a piece out of a puzzle or cut a hole in a piece of cloth, my intuition is what would know how to fill that piece in the puzzle, or fix the hole in the cloth. You may be seeking throughout your whole lifetime, using traditional methods, the only methods you know, to find the piece of the puzzle, or that missing piece of cloth but you are seeking these in areas where they do not exist. Yet the pieces do exist—in the omnipotent power of the unconscious mind. When you combine your subconscious with your intuition, it will direct you to exactly where you can find the missing piece of the puzzle, or piece of the cloth, or the filling that goes into the void in your life. And only as a holistic being are you able to serve yourself and others at your maximum capacity.

By filling the void of emotion, love, and everything outside the insatiable ego, you can create a whole perspective, based on the whole being of which you are meant to be and were meant to be from the beginning of your life. This allows you to utilize yourself as a sum of all the parts, instead of separating yourself and trying to direct your attention toward each individual part, which is an exercise in futility. Once you are able to understand that your true GPS is your intuition, then you're going to be able to direct yourself toward the favorable outcomes in your life.

When the individual mind attempts to penetrate the wall of separateness that stands between itself and others, then that individual must turn his eyes away from the delusive surface of differences and look beyond this veil into the inner core of his own subconscious and spiritual forces.

There will be many times, when looking at themselves, that a person will feel infinite and eternal based on their mental state at that time. The challenge is to control your mental state, so that it serves you at any time. To arrive at this state of identification with yourself is to know the purity of emotion and love and ultimately, oneness within self. The process will always be there to serve you. Look inside your secret heart and you will understand that your ability to create what you want is actually a simple process. It need not be complex. It is the lack of understanding of the process that creates the complexity.

We often take that which is simple and make it complex. For example, consider the bartender in a restaurant as he does his phenomenal work. He is filling orders, making two or three drinks at a time, taking more orders, handling cash, working the till, dealing with customers, and all with an amazing array of fluidity and simplicity. Yet, if you were to put me behind the counter, it would suddenly seem so complex. I would be asking what liquor do I use, what glass for what drink, what garnishes do I use, how do I use the cash register, and so on. It becomes complex, but in reality it is still relatively simple. Bartending, after all, can be learned in a few weeks and practiced to a state of mastery beyond that.

Your mind is the same. You can master the basics, which you have been doing by reading this book, and then accelerate and evolve these skills into a state of mastery. It will eventually lead you to encompass all facets of yourself.

A powerful technique when practicing intuition is to look at yourself in the mirror. The next time you look at yourself in the mirror, remove yourself from your physical senses, your eyes, and feel how you feel about yourself. Use an intuitive, non-judgmental feeling. Try not to consciously judge yourself (for example, refrain from comments like, "I don't like my hair"). Instead, feel that image looking back at you so you can generate that origin of self-love.

Self-love is fundamental to a successful, healthy life. However, self-love is dissipated as we move through childhood, by the criticism of others, among other things. We forget our true nature, our connection with Universal Power, the very fact that we are pure creation and beautiful and perfect. We become overrun with critical thoughts and programs running in our conscious mind that disallow this self-love. However, in order to truly love one another and contribute in a purposeful way in the world, self-love is essential. Further, once we're able to regain that self-love, intuition will push it out and create a reciprocal bond. In other words, we will share our love for ourselves with all with whom we come into contact, and they will feel it and love us more. Giving our love for ourselves yields more love from others.

Sometimes when I teach this in seminars, the whole conversation about intuition seems esoteric and far-fetched, yet once it is grasped and people become familiar with these techniques, often they become fascinated to the point where they are disappointed they didn't learn these things twenty, thirty, forty years earlier.

But regardless of whether you are reading this book at twenty, forty, sixty, or eighty years old, now is the time to begin living as a whole human being, utilizing your mind and the subconscious mind as your omnipresent ally. Once you're able to do that, you are able to live within love and use your intuition as a guide and barometer. You can create subconsciously all the benefits you seek, whether it's good health, financial wealth, or relationships because today truly is the next day of the rest of your life.

We maximize our presence and time here on Earth in terms of serving others and creating an environment that serves us as well. And I mean an environment that serves us by giving, I don't mean by taking. But you are more than deserving when it comes to living the life you want. It is an abundant world, and you deserve love, happiness, financial security, good health, all of it. Within you is the capacity to have it all.

So read this book, highlight it, then read it again. Read it again and again, until the information becomes second nature to you. This way, just like the seasoned bartender can be mixing a complicated drink while holding up his end of a conversation with a customer, you too will no longer have to think your way through every step. Your subconscious mind will create a conditioned response, and that will create a loop with the intuitive mind as well.

I know there are many psychics out there and it is easy— and all too common—for people to believe they are all charlatans. However, I prefer to call these people intuitives, and I know many people like this who have uncanny accuracy in their intuition. These people are truly in tune with the universe, consciousness, and the energy that exists all around us. For some, they were born with it already finely honed, while others did work on themselves and engaged in practice to hone their intuition to bring it to the level where they can use it in helpful ways in their lives. We are human, but we are much more than human. We are flesh and blood, but we are much more than flesh and blood.

We are walking individuals with the insertion of something called the human mind, and that mind is absolutely the most powerful thing in the world.

With repetition, practice, attunement, and intuitive connecting, you will be able to utilize your powerful human mind more than ninety-five percent of the individuals who walk this planet. And by doing so, you will be able to acquire what you want in terms of happiness, peace of mind, love, wealth, health, and everything else that awaits you as a whole, operating human being. After all, the ultimate goal for anyone who lives on this planet is the ability to leave a legacy of betterment amongst everyone with whom they are in contact. Through my lifetime devoted to learning about the mind and the creation of these techniques in this book, I assure you doing the work to master the basics will set you sure-footedly upon this path.

Part Six: The Arrival

Chapter Twenty: Are You Ready? Hold On!

Having read the whole book thus far, I am hopeful you will have begun to clearly see how you are the creator of your destiny and where you may be holding yourself back in your life. I am hopeful that you will have started to develop awareness of what limiting thoughts exist for you in a habitual way, and what emotional state you find yourself in most frequently. Remember, emotions are a major component of the operation of the subconscious mind. Instead of feeling like the life you dream of is impossible to reach, I want you to understand that you can build a clear path to achieving your goals. Now it is up to you to practice remaining in a place of knowing, through emotionalizing and visualizing your desired outcome, expecting success, and applying gratitude and appreciation to your actions so that you can build your own life by design.

Part of staying with this knowledge is being confident that the technology really works. I can assure you that it does. I can also assure you that once you really commit to applying these techniques and commit to making changes in your life, those changes will come about. You may not have control over the way the changes occur, indeed it is important to understand that the universe will manifest things for you on its own time and in its own way (this is why detachment is so important), but the changes will occur.

Which means the next step is being ready to let go of the old identity that has you where you are today, which is possibly feeling stuck or scared, and seeking a path to peace and prosperity. In letting go of this old identity, you can be sure the identity won't go without a fight. So be willing to recognize it when it comes and don't get sucked in. The identity will hang on for dear life and might cause all kinds of havoc as you work on your subconscious mind to create change. That's okay—recognize it for what it is, and stay diligent on the path of reprogramming your subconscious mind.

The truth is, if you have read this book, integrated the concepts, and started to work on the practical applications I offered, then you can liken yourself to a boxer who has trained, and trained, and trained some more, and is getting ready to step into the ring. The ring is your life, and the techniques in this book are the training grounds. The techniques are the punching bag, your sparring opponent, all of the work that needs to be done to ready yourself for your big fight. Like a boxer, it is up to you now to go forth confidently and with full knowledge and belief in the power of your training, with the expectation of winning. You can only win the fight if you are fully confident that you have trained well, and you know both your strengths and your opponent's weaknesses. Without self-confidence, you will not win. This is a critical piece of the foundation upon which all of the techniques and concepts I have explained in this book now stands.

It is exciting, however, to make change and shift away from old identities. These constructs have served you well over the years, protected you during your childhood, and allowed you to hold fast with the certainty of who you are. But if you are reading this book, chances are you are dissatisfied and you know that you need to make a shift. As you do the work and apply the techniques, try to stay excited about what is happening. I named this chapter "Are you ready? Hold on!" for a reason, and that is because what is waiting for you once you commit to change is an adventure beyond what you can even imagine. Your life is what is waiting for you. How big and bold you want to paint that masterpiece is up to you.

Face the dying of your identity with bravery and do not let it sway your course! You are the only one who can change you. You are the only one keeping yourself down. You are the only one that this book is for. The chaos of old patterns leaving you will settle the steadier you remain in the application of the techniques. You will grow stronger each day when it comes to choosing which thoughts you want to hold, and this will allow you to choose positive and affirming thoughts. If you fall off track, start again. Let nothing deter you from your goals and desired outcome. Read this book again and again until you have integrated the concepts and techniques. Be willing to put in the necessary work and be willing to stay with it, even when your ship dips and bobs and threatens to sink.

Be sure to not overanalyze the techniques or the work as you begin to apply them with regularity. Our analytical capabilities are a powerful trait. By these I am referring to your ability to analyze. Different people use their analytical capabilities at different levels, and it is important that you recognize how you use yours.

The ability to analyze is a double-edged sword; it is all too easy to succumb to 'paralysis of analysis,' where you find yourself analyzing yourself right out of a situation because you are looking for what's wrong about it.

I often have a laminated jigsaw puzzle with me when I do my seminars. I take out one piece of the puzzle, then laminate it and hold the puzzle before the audience. Of course, the audience notices the missing piece, and this determines their perception of the puzzle.

Consider it this way: When a child goes to the playground, that child is enthusiastic about playing and trying out the swings and slides. The child doesn't analyze the playground, wondering how the chains on the swings are attached, or are the seats on the swings wooden or rubber, or wondering how the swings move, or considering the dangers of swinging too high. The analytical mind is able to look at everything and see both the good and the bad. While there are advantages to seeing the bad, that 'paralysis of analysis' can occur all too easily.

Another example might be two people who want to adventure into unknown territories. Perhaps the desert, or the jungle. The person with a higher sense of adventure and lesser analytical integration will be focused on the outcome of their trip. Does that mean they have alleviated the dangers such a trip involves? No, but they are excited to go on the adventure.

The other adventurer might be overly analytical. This person will analyze the deaths that may have occurred in the area, or the potential for snakes or spiders that can bite them, or the weather conditions, or the outcome of what might happen. During the process of analysis, they are making a list of positives and negatives. This is common to many of us, to list out the positives and negatives. However, unless you are able to negate the negatives and move forward, you run the risk of becoming paralyzed and staying in a state of inaction.

Less analytical people in general are the creative powers that change the world. These are the people who hire analytical people, thereby ensuring that movement towards the creative outcome is met with least resistance.

Look at your own mind as a playground and a newfound exploratory territory you can go into. Try to summon a state of wonderment and anticipation—you've found a new playground, and it has been in your own mind all along! Experience a childlike excitation going into that playground, and it will keep you excited about learning your new tools.

In the course of this book, you've looked at several thought-provoking ideas, concepts, and tactics, so at least once every few days, close your eyes and go into the playground without analyzing it or assuming anything. Just go in there and familiarize yourself with the playground. How many times has the light been turned on in the subconscious? A lifetime's worth! So many people live in the darkness, not knowing of the Universal Power accessible through their subconscious minds the whole time, to find out now that so much of the stress they've endured was unnecessary.   You have the ability to access knowledge—knowledge that will come to you in the form of intuition, direction, clarity—you have that ability all within the playground of your mind. I like to watch people that are becoming excited about the power of their own mind simply lie down for fifteen or twenty minutes and go into that new playground. Little did they know they've had it for twenty, forty, sixty, even eighty years! Yet they have never explored it. It's like having the ocean or the Amazon right in front of you—you don't need to go there when you have a never-ending, full-capacity environment.   When you visit the playground of your mind with a childlike curiosity, you're going to find that you yourself are the most fascinating territory to explore, and you will enjoy every aspect of the journey

Here is a little gauge I use to check the temperature of the playground. If you were to think of something stressful right now, how long would it take for you to summon that thought? One second? Five seconds? Ten seconds?

Conversely, if you were to think of something happy, joyous, and loving, how long would it take for that thought to appear?

If it takes you ten seconds to think of something stressful, but twenty seconds to think of something joyful and happy, then we know what theme dominates your thoughts, and what the temperature is like in your playground. Whatever thought is 'closest' is the thought you can reach out and grab first. Whatever thought yielded the quickest reaction time is what moves those kinds of thoughts closer and as it does, it moves closer to the ability to be rebroadcast out in an even more powerful state.

Use that test on yourself right now. Close your eyes and think of a stressful thought. How long did that take?

Now open and close your eyes, reset your mind's eye, and think of a happy and joyous and abundant thought. How long did that take?

You have things in your life that are joyous, loving, and abundant. These might be your children, your spouse, your dog, or your hobbies, and you also have things that are stressful in your life. The human mind has a tendency to amplify and clarify the stressors. This is like creating a barrier in your mind that you need to walk through to get to the garden of happiness. You need to walk through that self-imposed barrier because you moved it there! You moved it right in front of yourself, and the more you think about it, the more it becomes stronger. Is it impenetrable? No, but when you push against it enough times, you become exhausted, so you just go back and retreat because you've created a barrier so powerful that it's not worth moving through it anymore. You become too tired, psychically, to move through the barrier.

If you are constantly moving forward with an abundant, loving, and joyful mindset, the stressors on the other side of the barrier cannot move closer to you because they can't get through this side. You built a new barrier by choosing your dominant thoughts to be those of love and abundance. Are you building a barrier of fear and stress, or are you building a barrier of love and abundance? Either one will insulate you from the other. Be aware of what you're building! A good way to know is the exercise we just did, if one type of thought takes longer than the other to summon, there's your gauge on what you're creating your barrier with.

Building a barrier of fearful, stressful, and negative thoughts leaves you open to submerging from time to time in a state of helplessness. One of the major strategies I teach my students when learning to use their own minds is detachment from helplessness. There is no such state as helplessness, there is only the potential to reframe helplessness as a bridge, or something to overcome as an absolute.

When looking at your own mind, once you revert to becoming engaged in a state of helplessness, your mind can't help you anymore. Repetition is the mother of learning, after all, and you will be reinforcing helplessness through repetition the more you engage it. The reality is there is no such state as helplessness, and in fact nothing is further from the truth. The Universal Power that surrounds us—as God, the universe, source, however you think of it—has the ability to assist you. There's your own mind that has the ability to assist you, there's the Universal Power working through your subconscious mind to assist you, and there's the integration of the two that has the ability to assist you. If nothing more than contributing to your faith of outcome, it is still moving you out of a state of helplessness.

Think of prisoners of war or people diagnosed with a terminal illness. Their ability to reframe their experiences in a state of perpetual faith is the incredible ally that moves them out of those situations. History is full of people that have overcome terminal illnesses and people that have survived in prisoner-of-war situations, or survived in adverse climates when they shouldn't have. It was all done by great faith of the mind, and if you wish to attach this faith to a higher power, that is even more helpful.

Detaching from a state of helplessness on any occasion is basically using your ability within to sustain the ability to overcome. This will allow the human potential engineered in the mind to create the outcome you want. Think of a situation where you felt there was no way out—are you still in it? If you are, then you have relegated yourself to a state of helplessness, because there is *always* a way out. One of the fundamental strategies for moving out is the ability to do, or tell yourself to do, whatever it takes. Of course, as long as we're talking about action that is morally and ethically legal, if you are willing to do whatever it takes, the mind goes into action with a can-do outcome based on assumption. Once you're willing to do whatever it takes, most of the time you don't have to do whatever it takes. The willingness, however, is paramount.

A good example of this was seen once through the behavior of my friend, Rick. Rick owned a nutritional company that he was very excited about. His company exceeded the growth numbers of the competition, including companies that had been around much longer than his. These other companies seemed to put barriers on their growth, while Rick did whatever he could—*whatever it took*—to grow his business.

Here is an example of Rick's willingness to do whatever it takes to succeed in business. Rick had a new label created for one of his products, and once it was done he hopped into his car and drove two hours through Southern California traffic in the middle of the day just to see this label on the product. Just to see it! Could the label have been emailed to him? Absolutely. Rick drove there because of the *excitation* he felt at the thought of actually looking at the label on the bottle. Rick didn't even think for a split second that it was the worst time of day to go to Los Angeles, that traffic would be so heavy. I ask you, what would another person do? Chances are pretty high another person might say, "I'm willing to do what it takes, but is there traffic today? Oh no, that traffic will be bad, I don't know if I want to go. Let me find out what the easiest way is."

When you condition your mind to look for the easiest way to do things, you have conditioned your mind away from doing whatever it takes. When you're willing to do whatever it takes, and you are focused on the excitation of the outcome, you transmute any stress and fear in that moment. Do you know how much stress Rick felt as he went to Los Angeles that afternoon? Zero! His mind did not even for a second entertain the gas, the traffic, the hassle, or the frustration. His mind was focused on seeing his new product, with the new label. He wanted to hold the product, and when he finally did so, he became experientially engaged in the process. By becoming experientially engaged, his subconscious mind became emotionalized on the outcome of sales and, of course, this began to synchronize with his goals, and sure enough, his company exploded! Rick could have found many stressful things to attach to that trip to LA, but he had made a pact with himself that he would do whatever it takes to hit his goal, and he followed through on his commitment.

It's not unlike if you were to walk into the gym and tell the trainer, "I want to get into the best shape of my life, and I am willing to do whatever it takes." This means you've made a contract to do whatever it takes. There's no evaluation of process, or analysis. You will do what the trainer tells you to do, and your outcome is already predetermined based on the contract you made with yourself going in.

Contrast this experience with someone else who may also go to the gym and say to the trainer, "I want to get into shape, but I don't like running on the treadmill, I don't like lifting anything over my head, I hate abdominal exercises, and I really don't like pulling anything with a cable attached to it!" This person has put so many conditions on their success that they would be lucky if they ever got in any shape!

Are you putting conditions on your success? Are you putting tight criteria on your success with finances, relationships, or your health? Or are you adopting a "whatever it takes" attitude toward what you are doing?

I remember once reading a story about two gentlemen who both worked for the same company in Pittsburgh. One day, one gentleman said to the other, "I'm moving to Florida to live on the beach." The other fellow says to him, "How did you manage that?" to which the first gentleman answered, "I just decided." Well, the second fellow of course fired a barrage of questions and comments at the first man: "What about your kids? You will have to pull them out of school! You will have to sell the house! You will have to buy another house! You will have to relocate your family! What about all your expenses?" and on and on he went. The first man replied, "What about it? I've made a decision to do it and a decision to do whatever it takes to get there." The reality is, the second fellow was just as free to move to the beach anytime, but he didn't. Instead, he sat and dreamed of living on the beach. Nothing was stopping him other than the perceived inconvenience, hassle, and expense. When you are willing to do whatever it takes, you will deal with the hassle and expense and anything else that comes up.

Adopt a whatever-it-takes attitude, pull in your strongest ally—the subconscious mind—and the world is truly your oyster. You can do, have, and be anything you want anywhere you want whenever you want—all you have to do is get in self-alignment.

When you start to apply the strategies and techniques outlined in previous chapters, and combine these with a whatever-it-takes attitude, in any area of your life, be it health, wealth, or relationships, you can expect to see drastic changes. Do not set a time limit; rather, be open to things happening as they unfold. Remember that things manifest through circumstances and coincidences. Open your eyes to all that is around you each day and notice in every moment how things are shifting. You will see the changes you are capable of making if you release control over exactly how it should look and when it should happen. You can get that Mercedes-Benz, but be open to letting go of the exact way that you will get it. The universe works in unfathomable yet incredibly supportive ways, and always in its own time.

Many students I have worked with often say to me at the end of a seminar, "I wish I would have learned what you teach years ago." To these students, I remind them that their lives have certainly not been wasted up until this point. What they have done is acquired information and experience, and all of it is now ammunition for using their new weapon for success (namely, what they learned in my seminar!). To those of you who might be of the same mindset as these students, I say don't worry about needing to have certain amounts of concentration power. What will happen once you start in with this work is that you will start to understand that as you develop your subconscious mind programming mechanism, it will eventually become a conditioned response that you will be able to use in your life. Truly, with dedicated practice and integration of this work, it will become as easy as flipping a switch.

A great philosopher once said we never really live. This is because of our constant concern about past and worry for the future. Living this "would have/ could have/ should have" thought pattern, combined with worry for the future, is an extremely limiting use of our mental capacities. We worry about a point in the future, and once we've arrived there we worry about another point, until pretty soon we're at the end of our life and we have never fully experienced mental oneness with ourselves. Using the tactics in this book will change this—and, I would argue, we can then challenge that great philosopher, perhaps even create a new adage, one about how we live fully in every moment.

There is an acronym I like to use called A.O.M.A. This stands for All Out Massive Action. All Out Massive Action is the catalyst that will move you forward immediately in your life. Whether you are using your subconscious mind to enhance your communication skills or to draw to you that which you desire, All Out Massive Action gives a real boost of momentum. All Out Massive Action provides psychological reinforcement, and breeds excitement and anticipation, which in turn fuels and emotionalizes that which you are programming into your subconscious mind. Think of a car going a hundred miles an hour. This car is much harder to stop, or even slow down, than a car going ten miles an hour. You can put an obstacle in front of a car going a hundred miles an hour and the car will just roll right over it. Put an obstacle in front of the car going ten miles an hour and maybe the car will stop. The car stopping is the same as your own excitement abating, and this is when doubt sets in and you need to regain momentum.

All Out Massive Action also creates the energetic response of a draw. All Out Massive Action-oriented people are drawn to people of action, and they have been throughout history. They are not drawn to people who are sedentary or complacent. All Out Massive Action creates psychological anticipation, draws people to you in a real sense, and also creates a group energy effect that you can leverage or exponentially grow. That's why we see people get completely committed, to the point of being almost obsessive-compulsive in their endeavors. For these people, the obstacles appear to just move out of the way. That's because these people have momentum now, and they are engaged in moving the obstacles out of their way. They have also gained the assistance and help of the power of their minds as an ally on their journey.

The simplicity of the techniques and strategies shared in this book for use in the playground of your mind makes them accessible and applicable to anyone. Anyone can apply these techniques, regardless of who you are and where you are at on the journey. Be grateful that you encountered this book when you did, for it is truly never too late to make change in your life. Start to believe that anything is possible, and anything will be. Know that you are the creator of your reality, and step into that role with more self-confidence and less fear. I've said it before and I'll say it again: Today is the first day of the rest of your life.

Conclusion

When you start using the strategies in this book, you have arrived at your new beginning. Keep in mind, however, that this new beginning is not the summit. Think of it more like base camp, where you set up camp and get ready to go for the summit. This book and the techniques given in this book, if used properly and diligently, are like all of the training and preparation that gets you to base camp. Now, with continued work and persistent application, you can start to make your way to the summit.

Whatever your goal in life is, it is like the flag at the summit of the mountain. It is an uphill journey, and you will encounter challenges along the way. Remember how we talked about the importance of the struggle, as part of the process of becoming. You will be challenged by external realities, for example your financial situation, but don't be fooled into thinking they are outside of you. Now you have the knowledge that your external reality is but a manifestation of your internal reality. Now you have the tools to refabricate your external reality through redirecting your internal reality. As you make your way up the mountain, you may encounter obstacles to the physical challenge, but remain confident that you have the mental and emotional capabilities of meeting any challenge on the physical plane.

The challenges you face on the way to the summit might appear as self-doubt, fear, or lack of encouragement, to name a few. It is up to you to face each challenge as it comes and defeat the challenge through your own understanding and application of these techniques, along with your strength of conviction to stay on this path. You must apply the tools that have been given to you earlier in the book. The work of reprogramming your subconscious mind is not done in twenty-one days. You can expect this to be a lifelong path you are embarking upon. The fact that this approach is not a quick-fix solution is precisely what makes it so long-lasting and sustainable in its effects.

The uphill difficulties you face as you try to summit the mountain of your life are always generated by your own mind and thoughts. Earlier we talked about perception, and how our thoughts create our perception of our reality. Always. Regardless of what life throws your way, and we all have difficult moments where we are truly blindsided by an event, it is how you respond and react to life that affects how you live. The choice lies with you in each and every moment. Do you want to keep pushing up the mountain to reach your flag? Or do you want to go back down to base camp, where everyone is comfortable but no one is reaching the summit?

At some point, you will see that you have all of the strength, skill, commitment, and determination you require to reach that flag. You will also get to a point where you realize it makes no sense whatsoever to turn back and head to base camp; in fact, the work required to do that is more than what you need to do to reach the summit. If you practice these techniques, and attend my seminars and workshops, your wisdom on the topic will grow and expand.

The more you invest in yourself and take this work seriously, the faster you will reach the summit.

It is no longer a secret, not that it ever truly was, that our thoughts create our reality and that we can control and manage our thoughts. The subconscious mind is your vein of gold, that limitless and ever present access point to Universal Power. Use this knowledge, take advantage of what you've learned, and let yourself receive the support of this truly expansive and endless wealth of wisdom, energy, and omnipotent power. You can now see where you may have received limiting beliefs imprinted upon you by figures you grew up with, taking on their stories as your own, and, now that you know this, you can begin to work to step out from under their spell. From reading through this book, you have gained access to strategies and techniques that have been uniquely crafted over time from my own decades of experience in the field. Remember to use the Rules of the Mind in concert with the Universal Laws to deepen the implementation. Don't forget to amplify the power of these techniques through emotionalizing your thoughts. You can control your environments—internal, external, spatial, incremental—and use this to your advantage as you deepen your journey into this work.

Call upon your skill and resources now, after reading this book, in learning and applying these techniques, and let these bolster you as you push for the summit, the life goal you seek. Good health, great relationships, and financial abundance are all yours for the taking. It is only a matter of shifting thoughts, tapping into the power of the subconscious mind, and practice, practice, practice.

Mountain climbers are able to make their last push through high altitude because their bodies know what is required. Your mind and the muscles of your mind will also, over time, know what is required and will be able to get you to new heights thanks to your strengthening them.

Self-love will be paramount on this journey to the summit. Indeed, as any real mountain climber will tell you, one simply cannot make such a journey if one has any kind of disdain or lack of respect for self. Your ability to love yourself will allow you to master the steps even faster, and thereby increase your charisma and ultimately access your intuition on a far deeper level.

Now you have tools to start creating your life masterpiece, and manifesting great change on every level of your life. Stay focused on your goals and stay present with your thoughts so you can choose the thoughts to hold and bring you to prosperity. The journey and the destination are ultimately the same; the climb uphill just as rewarding as reaching the flag at the summit.

Anything you desire, you can create for yourself. If you use the techniques shared in this book, you will see shifts in your life, of this I have no doubt. You are a part of the Universal Power. You are here to continue to create and expand and to be successful. Indeed, it is your birthright. You will always be supported when you stay aware of your thoughts and persist in choosing to hold only the positive thoughts. Step fully into the limitlessness afforded you when you access Universal Power, and let that propel you forward into the great prosperity you were born to receive.

CPSIA information can be obtained
at www.ICGtesting.com
Printed in the USA
FSHW01n1821270918
52355FS